Behaviour Recovery

Bill Rogers

Paul Chapman Publishing

Contents

Preface to the second edition

This is a new edition of *Behaviour Recovery*. There has been significant revision and amendment of the first edition, while retaining the central model of behaviour recovery with its emphasis on teaching behaviour concerning children with emotional and behavioural disorders (EBD).

I have been encouraged by many colleagues in Australia, New Zealand and the United Kingdom, who have successfully used the concepts and skills in this book. I have incorporated a number of new case examples from those schools in this edition.

The new sections in the text notably address what schools can significantly affect with respect to that small percentage of children with challenging and EBD behaviours. These children have many factors in their lives that affect their behaviour over which schools have limited control. This book acknowledges the challenge and explores the practical realities, options and programmes that teachers are using to address that challenge.

The issue of attention deficit disorder (ADD) has been addressed at some length, particularly with older primary age children (and those in lower secondary). Issues relating to task avoidance, task-focus and organisation are addressed within the behaviour recovery model.

A number of issues have been expanded or redeveloped, particularly the issue of discipline and behaviour management (see Chapter 6). There is a perception among some teachers that the discipline of children with emotional and behavioural disorders needs to be different from children in the so-called 'normal range of behaviour'. I am not convinced of this. The discipline practices covered here are relevant for all children in all contexts. Coupled with the Behaviour Recovery programme itself, they provide the secure and positive guidance children need in their overall learning at school.

Children with EBD often present with poor coping skills, and frustration in learning, play and relationships. In this edition the issue of frustration and anger has been re-addressed with case examples that focus on the *skills* of frustration tolerance management.

Behaviour Recovery is most successful when it engages with school-wide collegial support. A whole-school approach gives the teacher(s) and parent(s) who work with the child the assurance of shared guidance, and the appropriate support necessary for success with the programme. This edition explores the nature and practical extent of colleague support when working with challenging and EBD behaviours.

While the Behaviour Recovery programme was originally geared for primary-aged students, the principles, practices and skills of the programme have been used widely in secondary schools, notably the middle years.

I trust that this new edition will prove a practical and workable resource to teachers who work daily to support children with EBD.

Acknowledgements

Many teachers have shared experiences of behaviour recovery concepts as developed with their students. These teachers have taught me a lot about how to work more successfully with children who have behaviour disorders. Some of their experiences with behaviour recovery are shared in this book. Few people have original ideas; I don't. I've read widely, discussed widely, and utilised the approaches in this book with my colleagues and found these to be a very helpful way of teaching behaviour. I have appreciated, too, the many schools who have allowed me to work with them as a consultant, and the children who have experienced successful changes in their behaviour at school as a result.

ACER have, as always, been consistently supportive of the project. My thanks to Ian Fraser, John King and Barbara Burton in the first edition; and to Anne Peterson and Joy Whitton who supported the second edition project. A big ta. Grateful thanks are also extended to Christine Kuszla who patiently typed up the final text.

A number of people kindly reviewed the drafts of this book, but my special thanks go to Janet Sainsbury and Marg Riley who encouraged me to go for it! Colleague support in practice.

Our oldest daughter contributed artwork to the text — many thanks Elizabeth. Our youngest daughter Sarah often came into my office during the writing of this book and was particularly intrigued with the drawings, asking, 'Why do these children need them?' She often drew alongside me, to complement my efforts. Thanks to my supportive family, Lora, Elizabeth and Sarah for their patience and understanding throughout the project.

My thanks to my colleagues who have shared their stories here; obviously, the names of the children have been changed. My thanks to Helen, Debbie, Halina, Elizabeth, Stephen, James, Caroline, Kathy, Colleen, Samantha, Grace, Vikki, Cairan, Robyn and Sarah.

Bill Rogers

Definitions

Emotional Behavioural Disorder (EBD)

The term EBD is a general term used in schools to refer to students whose behaviour represents as 'frequently' and 'typically' outside the 'normal range' of behaviour of students (within the child's age range).

Attention Deficit Disorder Hyperactivity (ADDH)

This is a common term, that also has a more 'clinical' usage when a child has been diagnosed by a paediatrician (or doctor) as requiring (or benefiting) from medication to support the child and his behaviour 'disorder'.

The more common term used throughout the text is EBD. Teachers will have students in their classes with a range of behaviour disorders and named syndromes (such as Asperger's Syndrome — a behaviour syndrome within the Autism spectrum — and Tourette's Syndrome). The focus of *Behaviour Recovery* (in this text) is not based around a 'medical model', rather on an educational model: one emphasising the *teaching* of new behaviours within a supportive whole-school ethos. The Behaviour Recovery model does not eschew any reasonable advice, even medical advice for such disorders, but emphasises that students can learn to manage their own behaviour while at school.

The He/She issue

The reason I've opted for 'he' as the preferred usage in pronouns is simply because it is the most commonly referred gender in terms of disruptive behaviour. Serfontein (1990) notes, with regard to ADD behaviours (attention-deficit disorder), that it is a disorder most commonly affecting boys.

I've also tended to use 'she' when referring to teachers because kindergarten and early primary school teachers generally tend to be female.

Photocopiable Masters

References are made to appendix materials containing photocopiable masters (PM). The PMs are teaching plans that form a key feature of any behaviour recovery programme and can be easily adopted and adapted by teachers for use in their own classrooms (pp. 169–95).

For every complex problem there is a simple answer and that answer is wrong.

(anon.)

Introduction

While visiting a school one day I saw, sitting alone, at a single table in the foyer, a 7-year-old boy with an exercise book. He was abstractedly doing some work. I strolled over for a chat. 'How's it going?'

'All right I suppose,' he sighed.

I explained that I was a teacher and introduced myself. I asked if I could have a look at his work book. He sighed again, adding, 'Yeah ... doesn't worry me.' On several pages, Nathan's work had huge red crosses across it. I asked him what this meant and he said that his work was 'no good' and he had to 'do it all again'.

'That's what I'm doing now.' He frowned.

We chatted about 'his behaviour' until a colleague arrived.

I knew this lad's teacher. I knew she had found him a very challenging student to work with, and had difficulty in motivating his learning. Yet, here he now seemed reasonable enough.

It is fallacious to think that because children will appear as positive, reasonable people one-to-one that they are like that in the classroom. Or, that if simply given goodwill and time they will change into responsible, considerate people.

I hadn't seen what this lad's characteristic behaviour was like in the classroom. I wasn't there day after day after day seeking to help him with his learning and behaviours. I wasn't there when he may well have been calling out repeatedly, butting-in, task-avoiding, or rushing his work (messily, lazily ...). I wasn't there when he may have been answering back and arguing with his teacher.

Children who present with *frequent* attentional and task-avoiding behaviour; children whose attention deficit disorder may see them *highly* inattentive, 'fidgety' and restless, and making it hard for them to work; children who are resistant and challenging in their behaviour do wear down a teacher's goodwill. This is normal.

It was, however, very disappointing to see Nathan sitting *there* — and I imagine for some time — with a heavily marked work book. Perhaps his teacher had — temporarily — had enough.

I have worked with many students like Nathan, and with their teachers, to help them give a student some 'structure' for self-discipline; some motivation and hope for a change in self-defeating patterns of behaviour; and some longer term skills for learning and *behaviour* that will enable them to get more positive, hopeful (even enjoyable) 'mileage' out of their day-to-day schooling.

This is a book about *behaviour recovery*: helping children to recover those behaviours that most children (thankfully) seem to develop relatively easily within their school years.

Behaviour Recovery

Behaviour recovery is essentially a model of learning and support for children with behaviour disorders.

- It is an *educational* model rather than a counselling or welfare model (it focuses on the teaching of behaviour).
- It emphasises *the skills of behaviour and learning.*
- It focuses on what we can work on with the child *in the school(ing) context.* It does not 're-victimise' the child by overly focusing on factors we cannot change, such as home influences, family dysfunction, structural poverty and characteristic diet.
- It gives the child (and his or her teacher) a *planned structure* within which to teach, develop, encourage and strengthen positive learning and behaviour.
- It is a whole-school model in emphasis and practice.

Behaviour Recovery recognises the many demands on, and limitations faced by, teachers. Within a whole-school approach this model seeks to *focus the effect of support on teaching behaviour*, rather than on discipline alone — or even counselling.

Children with behaviour disorders can 'eat up' a lot of teacher time. Through targeted colleague support and individual behaviour recovery teaching, teachers are less stressed and feel more professionally focused in their support of the student (Rogers forthcoming).

I received a letter from a Year 2 teacher (seven-year-olds) about a little boy she described as:

> *... being so out of balance that he often spins off into chaotic turmoil ... (he) is a blond-haired, blue-eyed ... freckly-nosed little boy with wingnut ears ... his blue eyes are very expressive and you can usually predict his mood quite easily by just looking at him. His (attention-seeking) behaviours are too numerous to mention, but I'll list a few just to give you an idea.*
>
> *Instead of joining whole-class sessions on the mat, (he) goes down on all fours, finds top gear and goes for it; racing around the room, under and over the furniture, kicking his legs out (to catch furniture and make a noise). He comes back to the mat, briefly, to catch his breath — and off he goes again.*
>
> *He enjoys being an exhibitionist: he stands on top of the table with his pants around his ankles and does a little lower body shake. He breezed into the room one morning with the announcement, 'I had baked beans for breakfast' and proceeded to flatulate, loudly. He also breaks wind and burps and makes any noise that he thinks will gain attention at the most opportune times (and the most inopportune time for the teacher). He also steals and often lies. He has great difficulty being responsible for his actions. Towards other children he is equally attention-seeking with pinches, punches, pulling hair, scribbling on or ripping up work etc.*
>
> *But for all this there is a lovable kid inside. I'm quite fond of Matt despite his behaviour. The real kid is very bright and has a quick wit and sense of humour. Unfortunately, his home life provides little or no sense of security. His father is on medication for manic depression and his mother feels she just can't cope and will often walk out on them. She is, however, receiving professional guidance and that helps a bit. Sometimes they (the children) do not have any lunch. The brother and sister are older but they also have huge problems.*

Matt is typical of many students with behaviour disorders in primary schools. Most teachers can recount stories like this one. Unlike children with physical disabilities, these children get little extra teacher assistance or support services. When education resources are stretched, more and more is expected of the classroom teacher in terms of behaviour management, discipline and welfare provision.

Children with EBD are particularly frustrating for teachers, and those outside the profession have little idea how draining these children are in terms of day to-day management. While these children clearly have a right to learn and a right to schooling in a mainstream setting, their behaviour creates more stress than any other handicapping condition.

Helen (Matt's teacher) was able to work successfully with Matt, over time, to the point where *'he now sits attentively on the mat, raises his hand, and is quite a popular member of the classroom … his self-esteem is excellent. I can't change his home environment but he has felt safe at school …'*

What Helen did, as many other teachers whose stories are recounted here did, was to acknowledge the real difficulties Matt had at home, but she did not let that stop her believing she could help Matt *learn* new behaviours in the school context. Using a combination of behaviour modelling, utilising the support of the other children (through classroom meetings), applying positive discipline principles, behaviour recovery principles and colleague support, Helen saw productive behavioural changes in Matt. She notes, at the end of her letter, the impact of Matt on her life. *'Needless to say Matt will live in my memory forever.'* (Helen's programme is outlined on p. 89.)

Understanding Children with Behaviour Disorders

1

Teachers are key caregivers in the lives of children. They provide significant emotional and social security, especially for students with emotional, behavioural disorders. But they provide this care at a cost.

I recall teaching with a colleague, many years ago, who had a child with extreme challenging behaviour in her Year 1 class. Although he had an 'angelic' face (in his better moments) with curly blond hair, he often engaged his teacher in major power struggles over refusal to do work, pack up equipment or join others during mat-time. He was noisy in class and threw tantrums on a regular basis. Her 'support' included a homily from the principal on being 'firmer with him'. The principal noted that, 'I have no problem with him when he's in my office'. This banal observation underlines the obvious — that most students are generally not 'troublesome' on a one-to-one basis, away from their peer audience.

Teacher isolation

It wasn't until my colleague broke down in the staff meeting one day when discussing Craig's behaviour in the playground that any effective support was offered. It did not help when the principal noted to her 'Did you know what your Craig did in the playground?' When a student is disruptive in this area, staff should take the approach that it is a whole-school issue, not just the class teacher's concern. *All* teachers have a 'duty-of-care' role for *all* students when outside the classroom. The problem in this school was the tacit acceptance of structural isolation. 'He's really your problem.' While the staff didn't say this in so many words there had never been any constructive problem-solving with all the parties, or any offers of pupil-sharing (rotating him in other classes to give the teacher a break) or constructive use of time-out or remediation for the student concerned. This tacit acceptance of structural isolation ('It's your class, your problem') is damaging to teacher welfare. Even if the teacher is utilising ineffective management practices, merely lecturing or blaming is only going to make matters worse. Perhaps it is 'unconscious' — there are schools where the colleague culture is unsupportive; there is no significant awareness of staff needs (Rogers 2002).

It may well have been that the principal was unaware of the effect of his unsolicited advice (the teacher perceived this as 'lecturing') or the perceived imputation that it were somehow her fault.

Part of the problem is teachers' natural reluctance to share concerns or problems (with senior staff especially) for fear they may be seen as failing, or worse incompetent. As difficult is the reality that senior staff, or colleagues, may feel that if they offer support it may be seen as implying weakness — as a result no one is really helped. Teaching can tend to perpetuate structural isolation — but this is thankfully changing. More and more, teachers are realising that the only effective way to develop positive behaviour management across a school is in the context of a whole-school approach where colleague support is the norm (Rogers 2002).

A supportive collegial ethos

All teachers need to know that whenever a student's behaviour profile is significantly disturbing and at-risk for learning and behaviour (see p. 21), such information is shared and due processes set in place. This due process is based around colleague support and an acknowledgement that this support is *normative,* not a special favour to any one teacher. The throw-away lines, 'I'm glad I don't have that little _____ in my room' or 'If he was in my room I'd show the little _____ who's in control!' are not much help either. It is essential the class teacher feels she does not have to cope alone.

Building a supportive culture in a school is not easy — it takes time and will need to be endorsed and modelled by senior staff. It involves emotional, structural and problem-solving support. It may also include elective classroom observations and non-judgemental feedback as a way of gaining insight into classroom behaviour and as a vehicle for professional development.

Colleague support for teachers with students with behaviour disorders involves all of the following:

Bill Rogers.

Looking through the classroom window.

- A whole-school recognition that all behaviour problems are best dealt with from a shared perspective.
- Recognition that significant behaviour problems such as EBD need a team approach.
- Willingness by the class teacher to accept colleague support, and recognition that this support is normative and does not imply 'blame' or censure to the colleague struggling with challenging student behaviour.
- Where possible, setting up (and participating in) rostered time release for colleagues who have students with EBD. (This time release will be used to cover the class while the teacher has 'recovery time' with the student.) In smaller primary schools, behaviour recovery sessions (one-to-one with the student) are generally held in non-contact time. I have worked with many teachers who develop their individual behaviour plans with their children at lunch recess time. While this is labour-intensive — on teachers' time and goodwill — my colleagues note that it is almost always worth it.
- Support of withdrawal of the student so that the class teacher can run a classroom meeting if so desired (p. 89).
- Normative moral support and recognition that a child's behaviour disorder is not the teacher's fault and any workable solutions are always

offered on a colleague support basis. (This should be the emphasis from day one of the school year, especially if the student's reputation precedes him!)

- The provision of a forum in team or staff meetings (as well as administrative meetings) to review any behaviour recovery plan. Support staff can give their feedback here, especially if the plan involves playground behaviour.

- Availability of colleague support through classroom observations is also an important means of assessment and review. Colleagues observe the child in the natural setting (with the child's peers) and use such observations during initial planning and periodic monitoring and review of any behaviour recovery plan.

  Colleague classroom observations can also include the opportunity for *elective* feedback to the class/subject teacher. There may be aspects of a teacher's teaching, behaviour leadership (discipline), or classroom organisation that may benefit from supportive, descriptive feedback. Such observations and feedback need to be based on elective opportunity, to enhance *professional* self-awareness and ongoing planning.

- Occasional class rotation where the child (on a recovery plan) may be 'enrolled' in another class from time to time to give the class teacher a break from the daily 'wear and tear'. Even one class period a fortnight can help; a whole morning or afternoon is even better. It is explained to the parent(s) that this process is to support the teacher and class, and that their child will still be doing his normal set classwork. It is necessary to distinguish between classroom rotation and time-out — not that this is to be viewed as 'punishment'. It is also important that the whole staff has decided how, and why, such a process is to be set up within the limited resources of the school staffing options.

Causal pathology

On entering school, a young child already brings a host of experiences to a demanding social environment. His family shape, his emotional life, a wide range of learning experiences and values have already 'enabled' him to selectively interpret how best he can belong with others. Do his parents value reading, problem-solving? What is the male role-model like in his life? How are authority and discipline exercised? What choices does the child have regarding his own behaviour? How is conflict managed at home? What sort of things does he get attention, praise or punishment for?

In any 'Reception' class (first year at school) the variety of children's non-school experiences can be staggering. Some, perhaps many, children have predisposing experiences that enable them to cope successfully with the demands of a teaching and learning environment like school — others clearly have not. Some come from homes where frequent shouting, yelling, put-downs, screaming and 'guilt trips' are the norm. One day nice, one day nasty — this is significantly inconsistent parental discipline. Some children have to drag emotional baggage to school that carries the pain of emotional (even physical) deprivation or abuse. These children have no choice about such predisposing factors, about where they live and who they live with. They have little direct control. Clearly this 'causal pathology' will affect their behaviour at school.

Other children with EBD have quite stable, functional homes, but they too exhibit a high frequency of disruptive behaviour; behaviours frustrating to teachers and students alike.

What we can and can't control

There are many factors we cannot 'control' in the lives of children, these factors significantly impinge on the child's behaviour while at school (see Table 1.1 on page 11).

A child's causal pathology may be affected by family dysfunction, by structural poverty and living conditions. The family values (for example, 'race', 'ethnicity' or 'authority in a school setting') can also mitigate against the values and expectations at school. Even a child's characteristic diet and 'health category' can affect behaviour for good or ill at school.

It will not help, either, to simply label or blame unsupportive parents (tempting though it is!). I have heard many teachers (including myself) over-focus on 'bad parents' and 'bad parenting' — abusive, aggressive, lazy, indigent fathers; parents who are substance abusers; mothers on valium sandwiches — and so on.

If such blame then shifts to 'victimising' attitudes it can affect teachers' confidence regarding what schools can do to make a difference (Rogers forthcoming).

I also hear teachers say, 'It's not fair, why should we spend all this extra time teaching him to behave! He should behave properly! They should teach him at home!' *Perhaps* they should. Perhaps in an ideal, fairer, more just world the child would behave well or appropriately. The fact is he does not — at the moment.

I have noticed, too, that teachers rarely say, 'Oh, we won't do any remedial literacy with the child because he goes home to some 'awful place' where they never read, or take any interest in reading so why bother?' They teach (one-to-one if necessary) literacy *skills,* build children's self-esteem, work collaboratively to sort out the best programme to assist them. They don't (at least intentionally) abandon them because they live in a dysfunctional home environment. We need to apply the same mentality, attitude and approach to *teaching* behaviour. We need to be careful that our explanations for children's behaviour do not become excuses — excuses that the child is unable to change or the school is unable to do anything. I have noticed that teachers, or schools, who use the 'explain away' approach are the least effective in assisting these children. It is crucial that outside factors are not taken up and used as *excuses* — as if there's nothing that can effectively be done at school.

A child spends a third of his day at school. During that time teachers can provide programmes, options, a disciplined framework that can teach him alternatives to give a purposeful sense of belonging and increase behavioural control. Crucial to this aim is the approach by teachers that emphasises behavioural choice. If a child comes to school predisposed to making poor, 'bad' or wrong choices, behaviour recovery can assist, teach and support him to make better, and more positive, choices while still reinforcing appropriate consequences when wrong behaviour is chosen. The research by Rutter et al. (1979) has shown that school environments (even in difficult socio-economic areas) can affect behaviour for the good.

Children with emotional and behavioural difficulties have a *learning* difficulty. This *learning difficulty* is directly related to their emotional and behavioural needs. When schools begin to address challenging, disruptive EBD behaviours (also) as a learning difficulty then positive and meaningful behaviour change is more hopeful. (Obrien 1998; Rogers 1997, 1998).

Table 1.1

Variables which influence student achievement	

Within student
Alterable
 	
• Desire to learn
• Strategies for learning
 	
• Learning style (academic coping)
• Prior skills/social coping
• Self-efficacy/helplessness
  (perceived or real)
• Prior content knowledge
• Emotional intelligence
	External to student
	Alterable
	
	• Quality of curriculum
	• Quality of instruction/enabling
	  motivation
	• Pedagogical knowledge
	• Content knowledge
	• Quality and type of evaluation
	• Quality of learning environment
	• Quality and management of
	  time/content

Hard to change • Genetic potential • Child's *characteristic* health/diet • Perception of physical differences • 'Disability category' • IQ • Family income and resource (structural poverty) • Family housing • Parent years of schooling (and parents' perception of schooling) • Long-term unemployment • Mobility of family • Members of family (functionality) • Family values • Family history • Peer socio-economic status	

Adapted from Howell 1993.

Disruptive behaviour or behaviour disorder

Many children exhibit 'naughty', inappropriate, irresponsible, wrong, rule-breaking behaviours (I did!). Children with EBD have somewhat different behaviour patterns. 'What often makes these behaviours deviant, and the children in them in conflict, is the fact that the behaviours are exhibited in the wrong places, at the wrong time, in the presence of the wrong people and to an inappropriate degree.' (Apter in Morgan & Jenson 1988). Teachers rightly get annoyed (even angry) and complain about disruptive behaviour such as:

- *persistent* calling out, talking out of turn
- *frequent* rolling around on the mat during instruction or story time
- motoric restlessness (hyperactivity, seat-wandering and annoying others; constant rocking in seat)
- inappropriate loud voice in the classroom
- too much time off-task, inattentive, concentration shifts (easily and quickly!)
- frequent non-compliant behaviours.

These descriptions are heard daily in schools, the most frequent being 'non-compliant and defiant'. Indeed, this aspect of behaviour is more frequently the cause of referral than any other problem behaviour (Kazdin in Morgan & Jenson 1988).

There are a number of terms (or descriptions) used for these children: attention-deficit disordered (ADD), socio-emotionally disturbed, hyperactive, even conduct disorder and oppositional defiance disorder. While these terms can be used in a 'clinical sense', for the purposes of this text I have used the widely accepted term EBD (p. viii) to emphasise handicap in terms of emotional behaviour rather than emotional states as such. Schools have marginal impact, power or even influence over a child's home life. Teachers can, however, do a great deal within the school context. As Wragg (1989) has noted, disruptive behaviour is not entirely the child's fault, nor does a retraining, or corrective behaviour programme, eliminate the need for other interventions (p. 8). It is essential that schools provide appropriate counselling, community welfare and ethnic aide liaison, alongside behaviour recovery options. The key point to note is that while schools can directly assist, support and influence behavioural change they may have limited success modifying home environment.

Behaviour disorder is a term that describes significant deviation from the normalcy which can be expected from most children of the same age and under the same circumstances. Of course, a definition may also depend on who is asked and when, and the beliefs, attitudes and experiences of the 'asked'. I have had teachers describe as 'deviant' what other teachers describe as 'annoying but normal'. Definition may also depend on the broad client group of students' socio-economic factors, as well as the school ethos.

For the purposes of this text, children with challenging and EBD behaviour are described in terms of:

- frequency
- intensity
- duration
- generality of disruptive behaviour. (Is their behaviour the same for specialist teachers as it is for class teachers?)

When a student's behavioural profile is significant in terms of the descriptions above, and has been considered so by class teachers (and colleagues), then behaviour recovery (one-to-one) is an appropriate approach.

Attention-deficit disorder

While parents, with the school, should pursue any causal pathology such as possible attention-deficit disorder, it is important to recognise that any remediation will have to involve working with the disordered *behaviour*. If Serfontein (1990) is correct, up to 20 per cent of male children have some form of attention-deficit disorder. The disorder is evidenced in behaviours such as 'constant' fiddling, regular inattention, hyperactivity, high motor activity, restlessness, easily distracted, clumsiness, inflexibility, low tolerance to frustration and acting-before-thinking (impulsivity).

Paediatricians and psychologists can readily assist parents (and teachers) with programmes to assist such children, even with the inclusion of medication regimes. However, if the student is on some medication (as part of the treatment regime) schools still need to address the ADD *behaviour* through some planned remediation and support procedures. Behaviour recovery approaches give the child a framework within which he can learn new behaviour patterns to minimise the frequency and intensity of the disordered behaviour.

Medication can't teach

Corey was a seven-year-old lad. He was bright, quick-witted and articulate, but frequently in trouble due to his behaviour. I was asked to 'see if I could do something ...' I had worked in the classroom team-teaching (as a colleague-mentor), so I had observed Corey's characteristic behaviour in class time.

At our first meeting Corey thought he was in trouble.

'You're not in trouble Corey I want to talk to you about how your learning is going in class time ...'

As we began to talk, Corey quickly jumped to what he saw as a real problem ... 'You know what my problem is?'

'You tell me.'

'I got ADD.'

'What's that?'

'You know!' (He feigned surprised ... 'Course I'd know, every second male has ADD!')

'I only know about ADD from the "outside-in" ... Tell me what's it's like from the "inside-out"'.

He began to relate (as many students do) how his ADD made it hard for him to learn, so he gets into trouble (because he rocks on his seat, calls out, and doesn't finish his work, and ...).

'So what do you do to make things better, so you learn better ...?'

'I have to take tablets ...'

We had a brief discussion about Ritalin. I asked him if these tablets helped him to 'put his hand up without frequent calling out ... (?)'; or if the tablets helped him to 'look at, and listen to, his teacher when she was talking, or teaching, the whole class (?); to organise his desk space so it wasn't so cluttered (?)'; 'to think about what he had to actually do whenever he had to do *any* writing task ...(?)'.

He laughed.

'These tablets, Corey, may help you with your thinking and concentration ... That's fine ... you might need *a plan, though, to help you to make that concentration work for you ...*'

Medication (for ADD(H)) can often assist a child's ability to concentrate; it cannot teach him what to do with this increased ability.

Teaching behaviour

When children come into school they have to learn to socialise, share, co-operate, attempt learning tasks (highly focused tasks) and cope with frustration. They have to follow teachers' cues and directions, follow rules and routines, utilise appropriate manners ('Please', 'Thanks', 'Can I borrow?', put things back where they found them, ask to go to the toilet etc.). All these deceptively basic aspects of behaviour can assist the relative smooth running of a student's daily life at school. They can also affect his learning. Poor (and disruptive) behaviour is often associated with 'serious academic deficiencies'. Academic survival skills [such as] attending to tasks, following directions, working on or responding to an assignment, staying in the seat, and following classroom rules are prerequisites to school achievement (Morgan & Jenson 1988, and Rogers 1998.).

Behaviour Recovery works with children, directly, to develop academic, and social, survival skills to build the child's self-esteem and sense of belonging. The student has to learn to wait, take turns, co-operate and consider others. School is a powerful social arena for children to negotiate. Children with EBD often struggle in their social relations with their peers; they do not easily utilise the social and learning cues that most five- to seven-year-olds pick up from the socialising and schooling context.

While it is natural for teachers to complain about such children, it is more productive to develop approaches will teach these children:

- how to put up a hand without persistent calling out
- how to wait for a turn instead of butting in
- how to sit on the mat during instructional (or group) time (without hassling others, or rolling on the mat ...)
- how to stay in their seat for more than a few minutes
- how to speak more quietly (instead of using inappropriately loud voices)
- how to move around the room without disturbing or annoying others
- how to (specifically) consider others (basic social courtesies and co-operative behaviours)
- what to do when frustrated or angry or failing.

When developing any behaviour recovery programmes with children it is important to begin with a few behaviours at a time and not to overwhelm. It is also important to recognise that behavioural change takes time, and success is defined as a decrease (over time) in frequency and 'intensity' of the targeted behaviours (see Running records p. 105).

Children have different learning rates and respond to a variety of teaching styles. Behaviour Recovery uses a wide range of learning methods through pictorial cueing, modelling, targeted rehearsal, individual encouragement and feedback, peer-encouragement and ongoing teacher feedback and self-monitoring.

Table 1.2

Basic academic 'survival' skills: skills as behaviours	Basic social skills: skills as behaviours
• Lining up 'outside' classroom (without pushing, shoving, annoying others …). • Entering and leaving a classroom in a way that *considers* others … (the micro-skills embrace concepts of what *considering* others actually means). • Settling down in response to group attention requirements by the teacher (for example, sitting on the mat/ready for class instruction, settling at one's work area, 'four-on-the-floor' on one's chair without distracting behaviours …). • How to get teacher attention during instructional time (hands up without calling out, waiting one's turn, listening when others speak — without butting in unnecessarily, eye-contact). • Movement during the on-task phase of the lesson (this is an especially important area of 'skill', as well as social behaviour, for lower and middle primary age students). • How to settle to a task (getting the necessary equipment, using work space thoughtfully, 'four-on-the floor' sitting, sharing of common resources in a work area). • How to focus on the learning task, and stay 'on-task' for a set period of time (for example, teachers can use task reminder cards, see p. 75. • Keeping the *task focus* of the work (not annoying others by touching their things, silly 'hitting' and motoric restlessness). Use of 'partner voice' in the work area. • How to get teacher attention appropriately during on-task learning times (how to ask, wait and go on with another task until …). ·	• Movement through others' personal space (basics such as looking ahead, thinking about where one is going/what one is doing). • Respectful language ('please', 'thanks', 'can I borrow?', 'pardon', 'excuse me') when moving through personal space …. To use language that *considers* others (no put-downs or slanging off). • How to make a point fairly in a class discussion. • Basic co-operation skills (sharing, asking, turn-waiting …). • Basic assertion skills (age-related). How to make your point, or establish your needs, without turning others off. • How to express feelings like frustration and anger without being aggressive. **Note:** many of these skills will be taught directly through behaviour recovery plans, and indirectly, through normal classroom establishment, as well as games and activities that can be used to highlight aspects of co-operative social skills.

Lee: a case study

Lee, a kindergarten student, refused to join in with the rest of his group for activities, either in or out of the classroom early in term one. Although considered academically capable, his social skills were poor. In group situations he would sit on a chair on the periphery, kneel on the chair, then slowly slide under it head first. In physical education he would watch the other children but refuse to join in with the activities. Lee's teacher felt that if these social aspects were not addressed then more inappropriate behaviours might well develop.

After discussing these concerns, and the appropriateness of a Behaviour Recovery programme for this situation, the teacher went with Lee into another room while the rest of the class was at physical education. She asked Lee to bring in his felt tip pens and then she sat on the floor with a piece of paper. With no preamble she began to draw, knowing that this would catch Lee's attention (as he is a talented drawer). A representation of the class was drawn showing the teacher, the class on the mat and Lee himself in a chair. Because the representations were in stick figure form, the teacher thought that she may have had to lead Lee, but he was quite able to relate to the picture.

First, Lee was asked who the larger figure was. He replied that it was her (the teacher) and, when asked how she looked, he was able to pick that she had a sad face. When asked who were the others sitting in a circle, he picked that they were the other children and that they too looked sad. He was also able to identify himself as the person sitting on the chair. (Here the teacher wrote Lee's name under this figure.)

She then asked why did he think everyone was sad and he replied it was because he was not sitting in the circle. The teacher agreed that everyone was sad because not everyone was sitting in the circle. She then drew a diagonal line through this picture and drew a representation of the class with everyone joining in, including Lee, and talked about how nice it was when everyone sat in the circle. She talked about some reasons for joining in (such as seeing and hearing things and sharing with the class group.)

The teacher briefly demonstrated Lee's typical behaviour and modelled the new behaviour (the behaviour in the picture that showed Lee sitting with his classmates — his teacher and his classmates were shown with happy faces to highlight the social approval).

(**Note:** this feedback is essential as it includes the social reasons for appropriate behaviours).

Following this talk she drew several small boxes on the paper and explained that, if he sat on the mat with everyone else, he could put a tick in one of the boxes to show he had remembered his plan. She then asked him what he would like to do when all the boxes had ticks in them. He replied he would like to go outside and use the play equipment (along with the rest of the class). Lee was offered the chance to draw the pictures himself. However, he declined, preferring the teacher to do so instead.

With the rest of the class resuming from PE, Lee was directed on to the mat with, 'When we go back into the classroom and you sit in the circle, you can put a tick in the square. When the squares are all full, we will all go outside for a special group activity'. What was helpful, here, was the emphasis on group rewards rather than individual rewards. (This increases the child's peer support.) Lee immediately went and joined the rest of the class who were forming a circle on the mat. Several children (and a student teacher) recognised that Lee was sitting in the circle, obviously aware that this was something that he did not usually do. The next time that a circle was formed, Lee again joined in and so earned another tick.

It might be worthwhile to note here that Lee chose to keep his plan 'private'. It stayed in the teacher's office and he could go in to mark the squares off. The first time this occurred he wandered off to the office. After a few minutes, noting he had not returned, the teacher went to find him. She found him in the office looking forlorn. When asked what was wrong, he simply said 'I don't know how to do a tick'. (The things we take for granted!)

The following day Lee joined in with the next two class circles (his peers on the mat) and so filled the squares. The teacher talked to the class, 'I am really pleased that Lee has been joining in our circles. Because of this we will all go outside to play on the equipment'.

The following week Lee was on one more contract (several ticks) and joined in the circles with no problems. It seemed that he had learned the appropriate way to behave and was gaining the social approval of his peers. They mentioned the fact that he was joining in during the second contract and then accepted it as the norm. A gauge of the success of the programme is seen in the following incident. From the start of the year, as well as refusing or being unable to join in the class circles, Lee had withdrawn into himself and become quite defensive whenever he had been spoken to about his behaviour. Shortly after going off the contracts he was involved in an incident with a Downs Syndrome child who was being integrated into the class. It was ascertained that Lee was at fault, so he was asked to leave the group. The teacher was concerned about what this might do to his newly learned behaviour, but felt that the situation required it. It was part of the classroom policy and was a logical consequence for what he had done. Shortly afterwards, Lee was given the option to rejoin the circle, which he did with no fuss whatsoever. Breaths were released, jaws dropped.

Since then (mid-term), Lee has been a constant member of the class circles.

Halina: primary school teacher

Exploring Key Features of Behaviour Recovery

2

The Behaviour Recovery programme is set within a whole-school focus: it offers support for the student and teacher(s) alike. The key feature of behaviour recovery is its educational focus for behaviour change.

This *teaching* of behaviour one-to-one (or in small groups) concentrates on modelling, cueing of behaviour, rehearsal, running records, feedback and self-checking. The primary aim is to help the student to be aware of his behaviour and 'own' it in a way that respects the rights of others. What is essential is that the process is educationally supportive, not punitive.

These are important features of the programme.

- Early intervention support for the student as this increases the likelihood of the targeted behaviours being generalised.
- The provision of a framework for structural and emotional support of the class teacher. This colleague support is essential to the programme.
- Protection of the due rights of all students to feel safe, to learn and to fair treatment. The charge (sometimes levelled) that teachers have to devise special discipline for students with EBD is ill-founded. What is special is the one-to-one support *outside* the classroom to enable the student to behave more successfully back in the classroom. In the classroom the student needs to receive the same discipline as everyone else (see Chapter 6).
- Utilisation of student peers through classroom meetings and peer buddy support.
- Emphasis on the whole-school nature of the programme.

19

Figure 2.1 Teaching pro-social skills within a behaviour recovery model

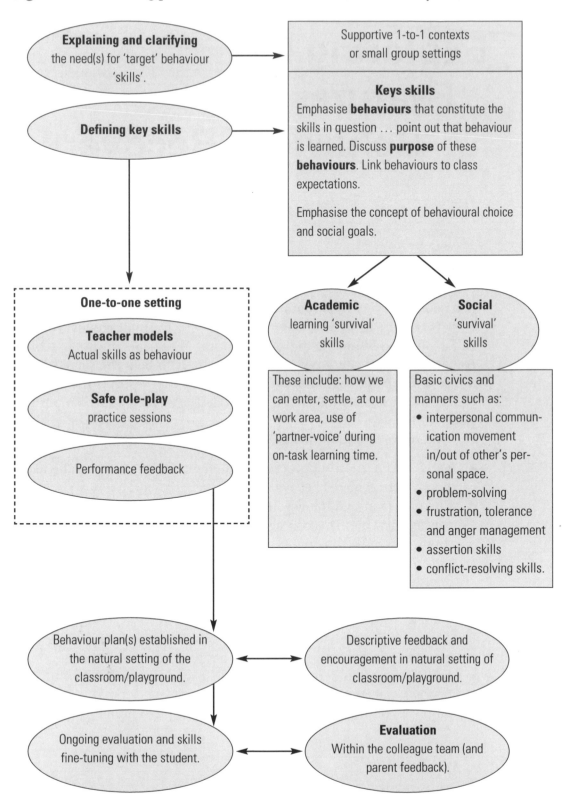

Establishing a behaviour profile

When considering behaviour recovery intervention and support it is crucial that teachers intervene as early as is necessary. When teachers note that a child's distracting and disruptive behaviour does not respond to the normal early 'follow-up', they will need to intervene with behaviour recovery support.

In establishing a behaviour profile the class teacher will ask the following questions. These should focus on:

- *Frequency:* how *frequently* does the student push in (during classroom entry)?; call out?; butt-in?; roll on the carpet (hopefully only at infant level!)?; task-avoid?; speak far too loudly during on-task learning time?; wander annoyingly (hassling others)?
- *Generality*: are such distracting/disruptive behaviours generally occurring across all classes or is the student 'selectively disruptive'? (Does this depend on which teacher or subject?)
- *Durability:* are such behaviours more than a 'bad-day syndrome'? Most students have bad days (so do their teachers!) Students with a behaviour disorder evidence distracting/disruptive behaviours several times a day, or per class period (day in, day out). If a student's behaviour is durable (over even the child's first week at primary level), it will help to initiate a recovery plan.
- *Intensity:* sometimes a child will display frequent and *intense* calling out, or task avoidance/refusal, or loudness. In such cases a time-out option is normally a short-term necessity. Time-out, while giving a student some cool-off/calming time, and also giving the class teacher (and her students) some respite, will not change the child's behaviour in the long term. Any time-out processes, indeed any necessary discipline procedures, will need parallel support or behaviour recovery sessions (see Chapter 6).

Supplementary questions will address:

- the typical reaction of the student's peers to his distracting/disruptive behaviours
- if the child's behaviour worsens, depending on which students he sits with
- whether the time of day is significant
- whether the behaviour is specifically more disruptive during whole-class instructional/discussion time or during on-task (learning) time (individual or group learning tasks)
- the length of a bout of attentional behaviour

- the way the student responds to normative discipline.

  There are many ways in which a behaviour profile can be developed:

- comparing notes with specialist teachers
- keeping a daily journal (bad-day syndrome or characteristic?)
- using a pro forma checklist (see PM 1 in the appendix).
- reflection on the teacher frustration-tolerance level at the end of the day(!)

It is important to keep some running records to clarify the teacher's own perceptions and to see (later) if the behaviour teaching programme has had any effect on frequency, intensity and generality of disruptive behaviour. They can also be used to share any successes with parents and can enable a clearer picture of the student to emerge.

Targeting the behaviour skills

The behaviour recovery teacher (preferably the student's class teacher) determines what behaviours need to be targeted. Essentially, any behaviour(s) that is (are) *significantly* interfering with the safety, treatment and learning rights of other students should be addressed.

Before the recovery sessions begin, it is important to specify the skill behaviourally. These skills will be modelled, pictorially represented (on memory cue cards) and rehearsed towards reasonable success.

Developing a behaviour recovery plan

The plan needs to be simple, achievable and workable. It should be one that addresses a few specific behaviours at a time. For example, 'Being kind to others' is non-specific. The child needs to be shown several particular ways in which he can be kind to others; the teacher then develops the recovery plan within those behaviours necessary to basic social considerations. With very young children even one behaviour is enough with which to start a recovery programme.

For an infant child, *sitting on the carpet* (during whole-class instructional time) is more than simply 'sitting on the carpet'.

When developing such a plan (for overly restless and attention behaviour) the teacher will need to specify (through modelling and rehearsal) the behaviours included in the deceptively simple basics of *sitting on the mat*. These include:

- eyes and ears facing the front, to the teacher, or 'to the board'

- hands and feet kept to oneself (no hassling others by touching, poking or pushing)
- sitting comfortably (this is discussed and modelled)
- when asking a question, or sharing a contribution, 'hands up (without calling out)', 'wait your turn', 'listen when others speak or share (without butting in)'.

Courtesy of Elizabeth McPherson.

Goals and targets can change over time as a child gains success with the behaviour recovery plan.

The recovery process can also be adapted to class work and assignment targets. Classwork is set out so that individual lessons are broken down to the sequenced and achievable — clear, simple goals for each activity until the child can cope with more generalised learning tasks. Memory cue cards can illustrate time on the task being broken down to three- to five-minute slots that the child can tick off or colour in (see PM 9 in the appendix). The teacher checks for understanding (by question and feedback) and ongoing opportunities are given (during recovery, one-to-one time) for practise of the academic skill within the plan (see p. 75). This demands a lot from class teachers. This is why colleague support is the essential factor to ensure success of teaching positive behaviour.

Role of the class teacher

Behaviour recovery relies on the development of a number of one-to-one opportunities with the student to teach him responsible behaviours. The ideal person to do this is the class teacher since she spends maximum time with the child. Furthermore, she can build in the encouragement necessary, for the 'take-up' (by the child) of the new behaviour.

Ideally, the class teachers will benefit from targeted time-release to enable them to conduct the one-to-one recovery sessions with the student. In small primary schools the only feasible way to conduct the one-to-one sessions is at lunch recess, or even before school (with necessary parent support). Care should be taken to emphasise the supportive nature of the time spent with the student — it is essential the student does not see such sessions as 'I'm-in-trouble-time'.

Withdrawal time

Ideally, time should be allocated in the last twenty to thirty minutes of a given timetable period. If a child is withdrawn in the first twenty minutes, then goes back in to the classroom, unnecessary attention is drawn to the fact of his 'special learning'. The student should leave quietly with the class teacher once the support teacher has established the class. Alternatively, the class teacher can leave to go to the room she will use and, once the lesson is established, the support colleague can then send the student with a responsible student (quietly) to the class teacher or behaviour recovery tutor (see p. 148).

If it is possible the first two sessions should be arranged within the first week (fifteen to twenty minutes with kindergarten age children). The number of sessions needed is determined by the student's take-up rate. This varies from child to child. Remember, only a small number of children will be in such a programme and all staff will need to support colleagues who have students in recovery programmes. A key feature of this support involves staff going on a support timetable (including senior staff — they will gain a great deal of goodwill if they do!) to take their colleagues' classes during behaviour recovery time.

It is crucial that *any* withdrawal time from class be conducted at a time when the student is calm and aware of *when* he will be spending some special one-to-one time with his teacher, 'behaviour-tutor' or case-supervisor. It is also important that the teacher minimise any unnecessary stigma attached to a child who needs to 'go out of class with a teacher' (because he's 'got problems'). One of the central goals of any recovery-type programme is to enhance and strengthen the child's positive participation in group life and learning.

It is essential that the class teacher maintains regular communication with any counsellor, ethnic liaison officer, social worker or psychologist in terms of the Behaviour Recovery programme. 'At-risk' students often have a number of people involved in their complicated (and dysfunctional) lives; positive communication networking allows the best service delivery to the student and allows for essential support for the class teacher.

Secondary level: 'case supervision'

At secondary level the key behaviour support teacher is normally a senior teacher who is given *some* time-release to develop behaviour recovery support for students nominated by the subject teachers as being 'at-risk'. When a secondary (subject) teacher has pursued typical early support with a student — to assist with behaviour — then a case supervisor is normally allocated to work with the student one-to-one (in non-contact time) to develop an ongoing personal behaviour plan for that student.

A case supervisor is chosen on the basis of their ability to communicate positively with students, their knowledge of fundamental principles of behaviour support, their respect for students' struggles, and their ability to be empathetic and encouraging. They also need to have visited the student across several subject classes to be aware of the student's at-risk pattern of behaviour.

The case supervisor employs the strategies noted in Chapters 2–4 when working with the student. The case supervisor also liaises with subject colleagues in the utilisation of the student's plan in classroom learning time. The case supervisor also liaises with other support personnel (school psychologist, psychiatrist and social worker) and, of course, with parents where possible.

While any student with behaviour and learning needs will benefit from the principles and practices of behaviour recovery support, it is normally reserved for those children who have shown resistance to normative classroom management and discipline in the establishment phase of the year.

Once a behaviour profile is clear (p. 21) senior staff will set up the necessary colleague support. This includes:

- the initial planning meeting (with senior staff and classroom teacher)
- clarifying and fine-tuning time-out procedures (p. 106)
- possible classroom rotation options (p. 8 and p. 113)
- the development and focus of the first behaviour targets within the behaviour recovery process.

It is crucial that the classroom teacher is given assurance and reassurance from senior staff, and that he or she will be supported through the setting up and development of any Behaviour Recovery programme.

Figure 2.2 The key elements of the behaviour recovery model

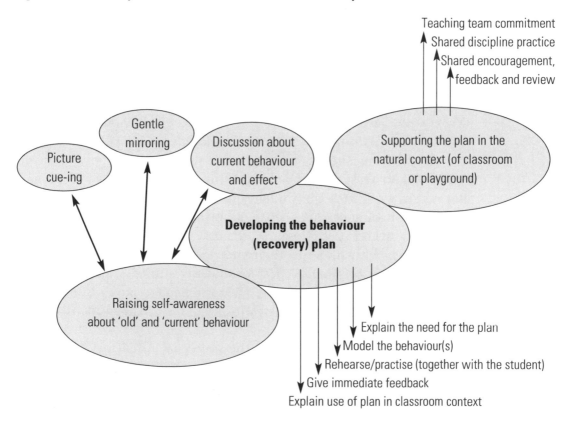

The one-to-one sessions

The purposes of the one-to-one sessions are to:

- Clarify the specific behaviours to the student and explain why these behaviours are wrong. Raising the student's self-awareness about his typical distracting and disruptive behaviour is a necessary step in developing any recovery plan. The child has to be able to 'see' that the behaviour is causing him to be unsuccessful in class. He may not know 'why' he behaves the way he does.
- Emphasise the effect this behaviour has on others (be specific).
- Model new behaviour(s) (the plan).
- Help the child to rehearse the appropriate behaviours so he knows what the new behaviour is and that he can do it.
- Encourage that behaviour in classroom time (or the appropriate venue for which the behaviour is being rehearsed; for example, plans developed for playground or non-classroom contexts).

After the child has shown interest in the plan most of the recovery time (in each session) is taken up with rehearsal. It is a labour-intensive approach but worth it.

With each set of behaviours the cycle is repeated towards a reasonable mastery (a significant drop in frequency and intensity of off-task behaviours and a corresponding take-up of on-task behaviours). Each plan is a framework for learning and mastering behaviour(s). Each individual recovery plan is often drawn up with simple pictorial cues (or digital photographs of the student), or a simple written 'cue card' with key points to assist the student to remember 'his plan'. These visual cues act as *aides memoire* back in the classroom (see the PMs in appendix).

Note: if teachers wish to use digital photographs of the student (as teaching devices) they should gain parental permission (via the principal).

It should always be emphasised to parents that any 'plan' will assist in their child's learning. We have found that an *emphasis* on learning, rather than disruptive behaviour, is more positively received by parent(s).

Some children respond very quickly to recovery plans — even dramatically — others take longer. For some there is regression before any sense of stability; for others the pattern is three steps forward, one step back.

The cycle of recovery for each plan normally follows this pattern (see also Figure 2.2):

1   Working for ownership of behaviour. At the first session the teacher can model the off-task behaviour(s) (mirroring), explain its effect on students (using picture cues) and invite the student to make a plan. If time permits the plan may be rehearsed.

2   At the second session the teacher goes over the plan again with the student using prepared picture cues, then models and encourages the child to rehearse (practise) the behaviours in 'his plan'. The teacher explains how the plan will be used in the classroom.

3   Back in the classroom the teacher encourages, supports (and, where necessary, disciplines the child) *within* the rehearsed plan. Any discipline is used *within* the context of the plan. If a student is behaving in distracting/disruptive ways the teacher will remind, direct or ask questions with reference to the student's plan. For example, 'What should you be doing now with your plan?' (See Chapter 6.)

I have seen colleagues in some settings (special schools) use the simple drawing (of expected behaviour) along with signing cues (Makaton) to remind and encourage the student *within their plan* (see Rogers forthcoming).

4   In subsequent sessions the child is given feedback and taught to evaluate his own 'performance' within the plan.

This cycle is repeated with each behaviour plan as is necessary and with subsequent plans. The teacher will normally start with a plan for one or two behaviours and work to other plans as reasonable mastery is achieved.

It will be important to explain to the student that other teachers will also have a copy of his plan (we refer to the plan as the student's plan: 'your plan'). Parents too are given a copy of the plan with an explanation of the processes and learning aims.

Developing the Programme 3

At the first one-to-one session (of any Behaviour Recovery programme) it is important to clarify to the student why he and the teacher are there. The tone at this meeting needs to be supportive and relaxed; chairs are to face each other and there is a table or two in the room. These will be useful, later, when modelling and rehearsal take place. As with any extended one-to-one session with a student it is essential that the teacher builds and sustains a climate of trust and support. It is important in this session the student understands that this time is not being used to lecture or punish him for wrong or bad behaviour, but to explain why this behaviour is causing problems for him in class and that his help is needed to work on a plan with his teacher to make things better. In order for the student to own his behaviour he first needs to understand it. Raising a child's self-awareness (about his typical and frequent distracting/disruptive behaviour — and its effect on others) is a crucial 'first step' in the recovery process. Rather than using long-winded explanations or discussions, the teacher will raise such self-awareness through picture-cueing and behaviour-mirroring (see Figure 2.2).

The child's self-awareness is further enhanced by modelling and rehearsal (practice) of target behaviours.

Mirroring

Children need to 'see' what we see in their behaviour. 'Mirroring' is an effective way to do this with the teacher modelling the off-task or disruptive behaviour to a student.

Ben: a case study

Ben was a residential student in a school for emotionally and behaviourally disordered students. He was very loud when talking at his table during classwork and loud when calling out to the teacher. I began our first 'recovery' session by explaining that he was very loud in class and that this was concerning the other students and his teachers because … Then I quietly asked if I could show him what I meant. 'Yeah, if you like!' he grinned, responding to what I'd hoped was my positive body language. 'Look, you be

your mate, Brian, I'll sit next to you here, OK? Now let me give you a demo.' I asked very loudly for one of the pencils I'd put on the table. (Ben was often inappropriately loud in conversational talk during on-task class-room work.) I then mirrored back to him how he called out to get teacher attention by clicking my fingers. I winked, 'Is that right Ben?' He grinned (boys often do). 'That's what I see you doing, Ben.' Here I'd returned to my normal voice. We then went on to make a plan for him to talk with a quieter voice in class, and to get the teacher's attention appropriately. I did this by showing Ben a picture of him speaking in an inappropriately loud voice and calling out with his hand up. A second picture was added showing him speaking in a quieter voice (conversationally) and putting his hand up without calling out. I then modelled the new (target) behaviour which became his plan.

The purpose of mirroring is to *briefly* model the behaviour so the student sees it as clearly as possible in a controlled setting. It's like holding up a mirror so he can see himself. 'This is what I see you doing — let me show you.' 'Mirroring' is purely illustrative — it should never be used to embarrass or humiliate the child.

My colleagues and I always ask permission from the student (as a courtesy) if we can show 'what it looks like when you roll on the carpet while the teacher is trying to teach ...' (or 'when you call out lots of times...', or 'speak really loudly during class work time ...') When the teacher has completed the mirroring it will be important to physically step away from the brief mirrored role to 'separate', as it were, the behaviour of the child (that the teacher has just demonstrated) and return to 'normal' teacher. The teacher can physically point back to the vacated kinaesthetic space and say, 'So, Justin, that's what it looks like when you call out lots of times', or 'roll on the mat during morning talk' or 'lean back in your chair lots of times ...'

One of my colleagues wanted to show an infant child how he frequently rolled around, and under, the small infant tables during whole-class teaching time (when students are supposed to be sitting on the mat — 'comfortably' — facing the front). My colleague got stuck under the small infant-sized table occasioning plenty of natural, involuntary, laughter from the child. Most students will laugh (some nervously, most normally) as their teacher 'becomes them' for five to ten seconds. 'I know it looks funny when I call out ... because I'm not you ... that's what it looks (or sounds) like when you call out (whatever) in class ...'

My colleagues and I have also learned to mirror what is physically possible. For example, a colleague was developing a recovery plan with a five-year-old who frequently climbed trees and buildings during playtime. While we wouldn't replay or mirror that behaviour, we could simulate some hand-gesturing to represent climbing trees.

Whenever I've worked with students on behaviour such as swearing or physically hostile anger (such as throwing chairs), I do not repeat the string of f____ words or throw a chair. It is enough to pick a chair up and pretend to throw it, or use the short f ___ (fricative) sound to simulate swearing in context.

We can also mirror the behaviour of 'hypothetical children': "Sometimes children do this when they are really upset, annoyed or angry — let me show you ..." The picture cues, too, will illustrate the anger, swearing or bullying behaviour (see PMs 11*a*, 11*b*, 12, 13, 16*a* and 16*b* in the appendix).

It is essential that the child has a clear understanding of what specifically it is that he or she is doing or not doing that is causing the teacher and other class members such great concern. One of the most powerful strategies for helping a child to identify a specific behaviour is to model that behaviour back to them. This process requires the teacher to withdraw a child from the class, and to actually demonstrate the behaviour. For example, say the behaviour is continual calling out or otherwise disrupting the class during whole-class teaching time. The child sits down while the teacher demonstrates what it looks like when someone jumps up and calls out loudly.

It can be quite difficult for a teacher to act like a child at times, but it can also be very effective. Previously prepared drawings can also give the child a graphic image of the behaviour. 'This is what it looks like when you are disrupting the class. Can you see yourself in the drawing?' A second drawing will depict, 'This is how the class looks when you are not disrupting their activities.' It is important that only one behaviour is targeted at a time.

From C. Breheny et al *Making Peace at Mayfield: A Whole School Approach to Behaviour Management*, Eleanor Curtain, South Yarra. (pp. 68–9) Published with permission.

Ethical probity

As with all one-to-one settings where a teacher spends any extended time with a student, there needs to be some consideration given to fundamental ethical probity:

- prior clearance and support of senior staff (as relevant to the ongoing behaviour recovery process)
- an explanation to the child what this meeting time is for
- a comfortable, relaxed physical environment (the door is open/ajar)
- if the student is an older female it will be advisable that the teacher who conducts any 'recovery sessions' also be a female. This is mandatory at secondary level

- if the behaviour being addressed involves the student *physically* hassling other children, the mirroring process should simulate how the child annoys others (by poking, touching or pushing). This can easily be 'mirrored' by simulating an imaginary child and the teacher becomes 'the child' annoying the imaginary (other) child. In this sense a teacher should not touch a student in such mirroring, or rehearsal, approaches.

It is important that the environment be as non-threatening as possible, with the emphasis on support not 'discipline'. Whenever we work one-to-one with children in behaviour recovery we need to emphasise in tone, manner and relationship that this is the time when we are 'going to work on a plan to help you with your learning in class'.

It is also important not to rush the key elements of the process, giving the child the time and opportunity to respond to the questions we raise.

Picture cues

Using the picture cue (see example below) the teacher begins by asking the child if he can recognise who it is in the picture (the child rolling on the floor ... or calling out ... or annoying others ...). To date I have never had a child not recognise themselves — they seem to instinctively know it is them.

The teacher then asks the child what he is doing in the picture.

Questions

When asking questions about the student's behaviour the teacher avoids simple yes/no responses or interrogatives such as 'Why are you?' or 'Why did you?' It will not help, for example, to ask the child '*why*' he 'rolls on the mat', 'calls out', 'butts in', 'wanders', or 'leans back in his chair'. Some very young children do not know 'why' they do what they do — even if it is for attentional/avoidance or anxiety reasons, or maybe for 'learned' power struggles.

Initially, it is more appropriate to ask the 'what (it is)' they are doing (regarding their behaviour). This is where the visual cueing is so effective as an aid to self-awareness. For example, 'Matthew, what are you doing in the picture?'

If the child says he's being 'naughty', 'silly' or 'messing around', it will be important to press the question (respectfully) a little further: 'What are you doing that's naughty?' If the child chooses or refuses to speak, allow some *pause time* and answer the question for him: 'What you are doing is ...'

- Briefly describe the *behaviour the* child frequently displays (not all the distracting behaviours), which is the one targeted in the picture/drawing (avoid describing all his distracting behaviours).
- Briefly note the social disapproval on the face of his classmates (and the teacher if a drawing of the class teacher is used). (See PMs in the appendix.)
- Allow some 'pause time' when asking questions — avoid rushing the dialogue.

Pause time can sometimes be uncomfortable; this will not be a problem if it doesn't go too long. Using our professional judgement is important here — ten to twenty seconds. While it does not sound like much, test it out.

Not all children like seeing 'their' behaviour displayed in negative ways — even in a simple stick-figure picture. As one colleague notes, 'When I showed Timmy a picture of him being disruptive (climbing trees

in the playground) he wanted to tear the picture up. When I showed him the second picture he was much happier.' (This is understandable.)

The focus moves to the second picture — the student's plan. In this picture the student is shown behaving appropriately to the context. His peers and teacher are displaying social approval — they are much happier now because ... Again, the link is made between 'belonging', peer-acceptance and fair, appropriate, *achievable* behaviours. It is often necessary with young children (infants) to prompt in reference to the second picture.

Referring back to Matthew's plan (p. 36) I asked what he was doing differently in the second picture.

'I'm just sitting on the mat, listening to my teacher.'

'What else are you doing?'

'I don't know — just listening to my teacher.'

'Are you rolling on the mat or hiding under tables?'

'No.'

'Are you touching other students who are trying to listen?'

'No.'

'So, what are you doing with your hands? Your eyes? How are you sitting? How are you listening?' (Allow a pause.)

These little prompts helped him to remember what was involved in 'sitting on the mat during class teaching time' and we discussed his plan afresh.

Children respond much more positively to the second picture — the 'plan picture' (their 'target' behaviour). The pictures also show the child's peers with sad/annoyed faces and often include the teacher (her face, too, displaying social disapproval relative to the student's behaviour). The message conveyed is that it is the *behaviour* — the distracting/disruptive *behaviour* — that the class (and teacher) are upset with because 'we cannot get our work done when ...'

The second picture (their plan) includes happy faces. This indicates social approval. When we ask young children about the faces in the second picture they always link their behaviour to the social approval indicated.

The first session will only be twenty to thirty minutes at the most. It should be enough time to explain, clarify, mirror and show the student 'his' plan. Finish the session by explaining that, 'We will practise your plan at our next meeting, OK?' It may be possible to rehearse some of the target behaviours in the first session, but if you sense this is 'pushing it' explain that will happen in the next session.

The teacher explains to the student that he will get a copy of the plan. If possible, in the first phase of a target behaviour plan, organise a second session within that week; subsequent rehearsal sessions can be spread out as support is available. What the mirroring, the picture cue(s), the modelling and the rehearsal do is provide several anchor points, as it were, to the student's short-term memory. These anchor points are all positive ways to support the change process, enabling the student to remember that he can do his plan (see Figure 2.2).

Note: laminate the recovery card (the student's plan) and make several copies: one for the student, one for other teachers and one for when the student loses it or tears it up in a fit of pique on a bad day.

After the 'bad day' has gone — we start again. Starting afresh each day is crucial to any success with behaviour recovery.

Modelling and rehearsal

In the example above Lisa is seen wandering during whole-class instruction/teaching time (she did this several times a session). During the recovery sessions I showed her the picture and mirrored her typical disruptive behaviour. I then showed her the second picture concerning on-task behaviour (sitting cross-legged and listening). Before I had a chance to get into rehearsal mode she said, 'You mean like this!' and dropped on to the mat. She knew what was required and why. The next step was to motivate her to want to do that! (see p. 40.)

Picture cues are employed to keep the learning process concrete and aid short-term memory. Students keep a copy of the picture in a plastic folder on their desks, or in their lockers or on the teacher's table. The teacher will have her own copy as well. Teachers don't have to be great artists in developing such picture cues, as the case study on p. 17 shows. Simple stick figure drawings can even be drawn by the child. Some teachers have used photographs of students in off-task and on-task mode. Some have even enlisted the artistic services of a student from an upper year, to draw the picture plan on behalf of the recovery teacher. What is important is the concrete picture cue card as a feature of the recovery process. Each 'new' piece of behaviour recovery uses one of these teaching/reminder cards (see the PMs in the appendix).

Below is an example of behaviour targets used in behaviour recovery with a Year 5 boy (aged 10):

- moving around the room (moving to time on-task and staying in seat)
- settling to and completing set aspects of a task
- hands up without calling out (and waiting)
- keeping hands and feet to myself (no pushing)
- keeping all (my) materials on my desk.

Each behavioural target card had its focus in a plan used over a period of time to 'recover' the above behaviours.

The double picture (off-task and on-task behaviour) is there to clarify, initially, the movement from 'old' to 'new' behaviour. This is replaced with single picture cards identifying only the on-task behaviour. It is the second picture that becomes the student's plan (reminder card).

Dean: a case study (Grade 5)

I have included four of our behaviour recovery contracts for Dean that reflect the target behaviours that needed modifying. Dean, although still experiencing many difficulties, has modified many of his inappropriate behaviours to the point where he can participate effectively in the regular

I can be kind and friendly to people

I can do quiet reading

calling out

I can put my hand up without calling out

I can work quietly

classroom setting. Eighteen months ago we wondered how we could possibly cope with, and support, him.

Not only were the teacher and Dean excited about Dean's achievements, his parents were 'over the moon'. They explained to me that it was the first time they had heard such a positive report on their boy in his six years of schooling. Next term we are involving Dean in small group modelling situations where they [the students] will be taken through role plays that will identify positive and negative responses to situations, and so further provide Dean and his peers with further choices about their response to given situations.

Jim: school principal

Rehearsal

The first step in any rehearsal session is a recapping of the previous session where the mirroring and modelling of off-task behaviour took place. The teacher will use the picture cues to clarify the target behaviours within the student's plan and then model those behaviours to the student. 'I want to show you what I mean by hands up without calling out ...'; 'What it means to enter the classroom without pushing and shoving ...'; 'To sit on the mat (without hassling others) ...'; 'To use your partner-voice during class work ...'

When I first began developing 'contracts' or plans with primary age children I made the mistake of just talking through the expected behaviours — many children would promise the moon. 'Yes, Mr Rogers. I'll be good for the whole time, I will.' I wasn't specific enough on what the expected behaviours were, I didn't check whether the students understood them and I never rehearsed (practised) target behaviours with them. This is a basic, but significant, mistake. Rehearsal is essential with pre-adolescent children. It enables recall and boosts short-term memory and motivation. It is one of the most basic principles of skill development and learning.

During rehearsal, it is important that the student:

- knows the specific behaviour skill, and its elements (for example, see pp. 15, 16 and 23)
- understands why this behaviour is necessary (motivation and need) for him to know and be able to do *this* behaviour
- practises the skill, gets feedback and support *while practising it*
- understands how the skill applies in the *natural* setting of the classroom (or non-classroom setting)
- receives encouragement and evaluation
- develops ongoing self-evaluation
- re-practises behaviour skills (as necessary) based on feedback
- is encouraged to 'hang in there' — reasonable take-up (even mastery!) will come.

Wragg (1989), noting research by Jorgenson and Goldman (1977), points out that 'learning-disabled children both recalled less and *rehearsed less* (my emphasis) than "normal" children. When learning-disabled children could be induced to rehearse they recalled as well as normal children'.

For example, when working with one older primary age child (Year 5), the class teacher focused on the skill of 'considering and co-operating with others'. This, however, was too global a goal so that student was then asked *how* and in what way he could show consideration. He came up with several elements (of considerate *behaviour*) that he could *practise* in rehearsal time and then apply back in the classroom setting with his peers. These skills included 'basics' such as saying 'please', 'thanks', asking before borrowing (and remembering to return) and considering personal space when moving around the room (that is, saying 'excuse me'). One could rightfully argue that these are *just basic manners* — and they are.

In behaviour recovery we do not assume — we explain and teach.

Figure 3.1 Elements of behaviour rehearsal

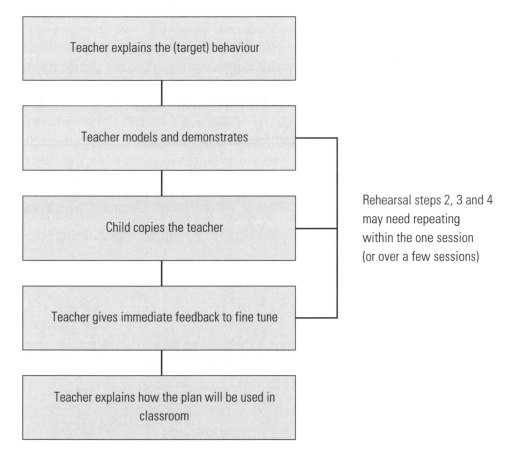

During rehearsal the student initially copies the teacher's modelling. Talk him through it: 'That's it, that's the quiet level of voice, Andrew. Now pretend I'm sitting here and you want to borrow my pen. You ask in a quiet talking voice — let's call it "partner voice". Off you go ...' During the rehearsal session the teacher gives feedback to the child and fine-tunes the elements of the plan. 'Do you understand what you have to do? OK, say it to me. Show me. Well done. You know your plan.'

One of the most common rehearsals my colleagues and I have conducted is helping the child to reduce motoric restlessness (seat wandering) and increasing on-task time. To enable the child to focus on a set time to stay on (and in) task, my colleagues and I use variable egg-timers (three to five minutes). In recovering sessions we give the child a simple activity (achievable) to do while at his desk or table, and explain he is to stay in his seat until the timer shows him 'the time is up'. Some teachers at infant level use sand (egg) timers or even the quieter electronic timers (that can be set for any time fraction). 'So, sit here, four-on-the-floor (seat on the floor). What side of the desk do you want the timer? Where will you put the plan (picture contract)? That's it, I want you to do this (the activity is explained) until the sand runs down (or 'the timer goes off', or 'until I come back to remind you'). Then, put your hand up (without calling out) and wait, I'll come and check your work, OK?' As he practises a three-minute task the teacher moves away (as if the other students are not watching). If the student forgets elements of the task it will be important for the teacher to go over it again a few times (most of rehearsal time is taken up with modelling, practice and feedback). With a highly restless child the teacher starts with the caveat that *when* the timer goes off (or sand runs out) the student can come to where the teacher is in the room and wait quietly. The teacher will then turn, check his work, take him back to his seat and restart the egg-timer for him. With older children, self-instruction (self-guiding speech) can be added during recovery sessions (see p. 57).

Practice

One way of challenging a student's motivation is to pursue rehearsal through a discussion about 'practising makes what we do better'. (Practice doesn't

really make anything perfect — just better, easier and normative.) People get better at something through practice. Ask the child what his favourite sport, game or activity is. How did he learn to do it? What was it like the first time? Who showed him how to do it first? How did it get easier?

Explain it's the same with this plan. 'This plan will help you to practise how to …'; 'My job is to help you practise to … (speak more quietly, put up your hand without calling out, stay in your seat, and so on) so you can get better at doing that … so we can *all* work better in class.' The teacher explains the reason for the practice and explain why it's important for the student *and* the class.

Feedback

When giving feedback to students it is important to:

- focus on the *behaviour (not* personality)
- give *descriptive* feedback (describe what the student *did*, *when*, …)
- be expectant ('That's it Dave, I knew you could stay in your seat for that time.')
- avoid overloading the student with too much information.

Feedback can also be given by mirroring. 'This is what I saw you do when you sat on the mat ... when you were trying to remember your plan ... Let me show you again what I want.' Fade the prompting until the child can do the task without fine-tuning.

Tony (Year 2) used to whine to get the teacher's attention and interrupt her with his work, demanding she see it immediately. Over several recovery sessions his teacher taught him to stand near her and wait (holding his work). She would then turn and say, 'Thanks for waiting Tony, let's have a look.' She would follow this feedback by directing him to go back to his table and his work.

All this was specifically rehearsed in the one-to-one sessions. The second stage (after successful take-up in the room) was to teach him how to wait at the desk with his hand up (without calling out and so on) until she came. To increase motivation she acknowledged him with an OK sign and 'Thanks for waiting'.

Privately understood cues or signals

Privately understood signals are helpful (and under-rated) primary reinforcers. Justin was taught to sit on the mat during instructional time (instead of rolling around). Whenever he did that he received an immediate 'thumbs up' sign and a wink. When Ben spoke quietly (according to the plan) in class time I would quietly say 'Ben', followed by the privately understood signal. Sometimes I would catch him looking at me and I'd return a wink and give him a 'thumbs up' sign.

During the rehearsal phase the student can be introduced to these simple cues to remind him of elements of his plan. These quiet hand signals act as reminders to previously practised repertoire. These simple cues can minimise overuse of verbal directions and reminders. Whenever the teacher uses such *brief* cues/signals in class it is crucial to establish eye-contact by using the child's first name, a *brief* tactical pause, and positive body language. For example:

- four fingers extended down like four chair legs on the floor (conveys the reminder 'four on the floor' for seat leaners)
- finger to the lips and the forefinger and thumb closing together (conveys 'Keep the noise down thanks')
- beckoning finger
- the teacher crossing her two index fingers (to indicate 'remember to cross you legs') and bringing her hands briefly together (to indicate hands in lap). She may add a cue to 'face the front', by putting an index finger to her own eyes and pointing back to the front of the room.

- OK sign with thumb and forefinger (encourages when the student remembers his plan)
- 'good on you' sign, thumbs up and out (with a wink this adds a positive reinforcement)

I often ask the student (in rehearsal time), 'When I do this (the cue or signal) what do you think it means?' Invariably, they get the meaning even before we practise it. I then point out that in class I will say (not yell!) his name and give him his 'special' reminder (the signal or cue).

Self-reflection

In subsequent recovery sessions allow for feedback on class performance. 'How do you think you went in your plan, David?'; 'What part of the plan did you find easiest?'; 'What part was harder?'; 'What did you do that made it easier?'; 'How did you change from ... to ... ?'; 'What did you do to help you change?' If using a tick-reward approach go over the ticked boxes, show him that he has been successful with his plan many times. Let him know *where* he has done well and those areas (specifically) where he needs to improve. Rehearse those elements again and add new behaviours as 'mastery' is demonstrated. The number of sessions depends largely

on take-up back in the classroom. Some children may need several sessions to stabilise even a few behaviours such as hands up (without calling out or clicking one's fingers), sitting on the mat appropriately or getting teacher assistance appropriately.

The child should be asked if he wants a copy of the plan on his desk, in his locker or on the teacher's desk. Most infant age children are happy to have the plan card on the desk as a reminder. Let him choose. Explain that during the day you will both look at the card to remember what he has to do in his plan (you will do this especially when he forgets). Remind him (positively) at the start of each day, and possibly after lunch recess.

Note: if using a reward schedule, explain that when he remembers and follows his plan you will cue him and later he can tick a box on his plan to show he has remembered. At the end of each class period you can have a brief encouraging chat and look at the ticked boxes. As the plan progresses over time, the ticks (secondary reinforcers) are given with more discrimination (make them harder to 'earn'). The reward schedule can then be phased out as the behaviour generalises.

Student resistance to recovery options

If a student is resistant and not prepared to co-operate with recovery-type options, there is little point forcing any elements in the process. Explain that you want to help with a plan. 'This plan is to help you in the classroom to ...' If he still refuses, let him know that you'll have another session next week (that is, 'keep the door open'). However, explain that if he continues to behave in these ways (here be specific) then, 'This is what will happen' (outline the immediate and deferred consequences). For those few children who use even supportive recovery time as a potential power struggle it will be pointless reinforcing that belief by threats or force.

Rudolf Dreikurs et al. (1982) note in their wide research on children's behaviour that such behaviour is goal-directed in the sense that children behave in ways that meet their fundamental social need 'to belong'.

Most children will meet this need, often in reasonably co-operative ways with teachers and peers. Children with EBD often use behaviours that may have undesirable attentional or power-seeking goals.

Attentional goals, in this sense, see the child drawing significant attention to himself with nuisance, clowning or 'smart-alecy' behaviour. He may show-off, 'constantly' ask questions, be overly shy/bashful or 'annoyingly' pleasant, nice and helpful — wanting to 'keep the teacher busy with him'. 'I belong when I get people to notice me a lot (!) and when I keep others busy with me ...'

Power-seeking goals in this sense see the child arguing, challenging and contradicting the teacher or using blatant avoidance behaviours. There is in such power-seeking a significant attitude of non-compliance. These behaviours, it goes without saying, can be very stressful for teachers.

Dreikurs et al. (1982) suggest a model of questioning that can help older children become aware of these mistaken goals and to help them focus on the *purpose* behind their disruptive behaviour. These questions (noted below) can be helpful when working with older children (middle to upper primary behaviour onwards). My colleagues and I have found it helpful to mirror the student's behaviour to begin the key questions (see pp. 31 and 32).

- The student is asked if he knows 'why' he behaves 'like that' … 'David, I've just shown you what I see you do many times in class … Do you know why you do that? Allow some pause time here (p. 38). This kind of 'why' question is the teacher's attempt to involve the child's 'private logic' about the 'purpose' or 'goal' of his behaviour. At this point most students shrug their shoulders or respond with a muttered 'no'.
- The teacher than asks the student if he can share *why* he believes the student behaves the way he does. 'David, I'd like to tell you what I think … I think that you refuse to do the work in class because you want to show me that you can do what you want — and that no one can really stop you.'

This part of the exchange can also be prefaced by the statement: *'Could it be …?'* The teacher does not accuse but suggests (through these questions) what the student's 'behaviour goal' might be. The question — statements below have been adapted from Dreikurs et al. 1982 (pp. 28–32):

1 *Attention:* 'Could it be that …
   - you want to keep me busy with you and your requests?
   - you want me to notice you more? Help you more?
   - you want the rest of the class to notice you?/laugh at you when (give a specific example)?
   - you want to keep the group/class busy with you?
   - you want to be special to the group?'

2 *Power:* 'Could it be that …
   - you want to show me that you can do what you want and that we can't stop you?
   - you want to do what you want to do *when* you want to do it — and that no one can (really) stop you?
   - you want to be the boss — you want to be in charge — the one "calling the shots"?'

Remember, the tone is questioning and 'guessing', not judgmental or pejorative, and linked to characteristic behaviour.

3 *Revenge:* 'Could it be that ...
  • you want to get back at ..., pay back ..., get even for ...?
  • you want to hurt me, get even with me for ...? [or] You want to hurt him (name ...) or her (name ...)?
  • you want to show me that I cannot get away with ...? [for example punishing, contacting parents, notifying the principal ...]
  • you want to make me (or the class or ...) feel bad or feel hurt?'

4 *Display of inadequacy:* 'Could it be that ...
  • you want to be left alone because you feel you can't do anything? You're afraid to fail?
  • you can't be on top, the winner, first?
  • you want me to stop asking you questions or trying to make you work?
  • you feel you don't know the answers in class and you don't want the other students to know?
  • you feel insignificant [explain] unless you can always succeed ... be the best in whatever you do ... or always get it right?
  • you feel you must never make mistakes (in your work, in sport, in school)?'

In pursuing the questions it is important for the teacher to pace the process and go through the sequence beginning with attention onwards. If the teacher suspects power (say) — rather than attention — it is worth pursuing the 'disclosure' on power. These questions form the framework for how the teacher could approach the issue of behaviour goal-disclosure. Dreikurs et al. (1982) give a wide range in their book. For example, take 'passive power' (what some teachers regard as dumb insolence): 'Could it be that you are not talking in order to frustrate me (and others) and make me feel helpless and defeated?' or 'Could it be that you are willing to do anything in order to feel that you can do what you want, when you want?' The hardest part of this process is keeping the tone of such 'disclosures' *supportive* — not being smug, rushing judgements about the child's behaviour (even if we are sure we are correct!) (Rogers 1997, p. 116).

• Most students say neither 'yes' nor 'no' in response to such questions. They will most often give what Dreikurs et al. called a 'recognition reflex' (a look away, a smile, a wry grin and frown ...). Some tactical pausing is important here. My colleagues and I often respond with a quiet 'I thought so ...' The aim is not to make the student feel uncomfortable, 'small', inadequate or to 'lose face'. It is a way of helping the student to know what you (as teacher) strongly believe is the case regarding their distruptive behaviour.

- If a student strongly says 'no' in response to the 'disclosure' (pp. 51 and 52) it will be enough to say, 'If that's not the reason do you know why you do "x", "y" or "z"?' As with all one-to-one sessions in recovery time the teacher's aim is to raise the child's self-awareness about his own behaviour and to give supportive assistance for ways in which the child can learn to change self-defeating behaviour.
- With older children we find it helpful to agree — in part — with their 'goal' of misbehaviour. 'Well, David, I can't make you do the work. No way. I can't force you. But I can tell you you've got detention. I can't "make" you stay back ... I can't make you do it ... Somewhere, some-time, you *learned to behave like this* (what I showed you earlier) ... Can you think of other ways to behave that will help you in class, David?'
- The teacher then invites the student to consider a teacher — student plan (the behaviour recovery process).

With any such one-to-one dialogue it would always be conducted at a time when the student is 'calm' (never in the heated moment) and when the teacher is calm. This approach, as any one-to-one approach in recovery time, is labour intensive. Teachers need to reflect, yet again, on the value of such targetted time (pp. 7 and 8).

Why should David have special time?

At primary level, particularly infant level, children will sometimes ask why such students have special time and why they have a 'special card' — with pictures (or a photograph).

If some students complain about so-and-so having a 'special card', the teacher can make a general all-purpose contract card for them (I've done this) and give those few students stickers now and then for keeping to the fair rules and acting responsibly. Or the issue can be raised at a classroom meeting (see Chapter 5). Most students will be happy that the student (in the Behaviour Recovery programme) is being helped to reduce his disruptive class behaviours.

Students will often need some positive discipline *within* the structure of their plan. Avoid 'why' questions in classroom contexts. If the student is not 'doing the plan' ask him *what* he's doing, show him the card and ask him what he's supposed to be doing. Keep the discipline low-key but decisive (see Chapter 6). It is crucial that senior and specialist staff fully understand the process of individual recovery plans and that specialist teachers, especially, get a copy of the student's plan and both encourage and discipline the student as the class teacher would. It is also important for the regular, classroom, teacher to receive regular descriptive feedback from specialist staff about how the student is responding to the plan in art or music.

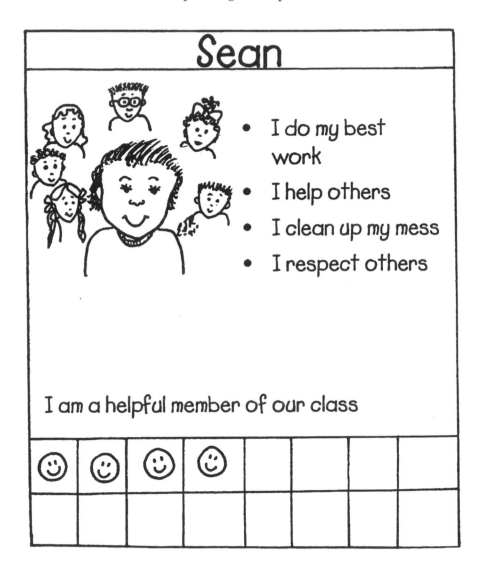

An example of a general all-purpose 'contract-card'
Courtesy of Elizabeth McPherson.

Behaviour recovery in the playground: a case study
Many teachers have used behaviour recovery concepts for primary aged children in non-classroom settings. This case example comes from a senior teacher who worked with an infant aged child, to teach positive and safe

behaviour in the playground. This plan was supported by the classroom teacher, the integration aide and the child's parents.

Tim was diagnosed with 'Attention Deficit Hyperactivity Disorder with inappropriate increased activity and impulsivity' in early childhood. Tim was in an Early Intervention class for preschool and was tested as IM ability.

In his kindergarten year, Tim had attacked children and teachers; climbed trees daily, as well as school roofs and water tanks. As Tim's behaviour escalated, he was placed on partial enrolment until lunchtime with a one-to-one teacher–pupil ratio. He also had an integration aide to support him in the classroom.

Robyn (the senior teacher) developed an individual recovery plan for Tim in the playground. In the one-to-one sessions Robyn used very simple 'stick-figure' drawings of the teacher, of Tim and of fellow students in a playground setting. In the first drawings, Tim was shown up a tree and on the school roof, with several children (and a teacher) looking sad. Their faces represented concern at the unsafe behaviour of Tim. In the second pictures, the simple 'stick-figure' drawings now showed Tim playing at ground level(!), safe, with a smile on his face, and the teacher and students with him also smiling.

'These pictures had been drawn beforehand as Tim's limited attention span would not allow him to wait while I drew them. He nominated himself as up in the tree and on the building, and identified the teacher and the sad feelings shown. He felt uncomfortable with these pictures initially and wanted to tear them up; however, when shown the second pictures, Tim was very happy with the result. These pictures were shown five minutes before play recess and for the first time Tim did not climb anything. The pictures were also displayed in Tim's room and referred to occasionally. In five weeks Tim had only climbed once and came down immediately when asked by a duty teacher.

'Tim's "plan" was available to all teachers when on playground duty. Simple, brief, corrective reminders were used if (and when) Tim was up on a roof (or tree). These reminders were to briefly help him to remember his "safe-play-plan". He was also encouraged by teachers when he was playing safely.

'Recently, during religious education Tim sat entranced as the Minister told the class that "if you climb trees you can see God!" At least that's what Tim thought the Minister had said as he recounted the story of Jesus and Zacchaeus (in Luke 19), where a short tax collector climbs a tree to see Jesus. He even had to colour-in a boy in a tree. Tim's class teacher could not

remove him that day from a return to tree climbing, and needless to say Tim has been climbing trees, basketball posts and buildings since!

'A few days after the momentous religion lesson, Tim was on the computer working with his Teacher Aide Special. He excitedly called out to his teacher that "they had found Jesus on the computer". Both adults emphasised that there was no need to climb trees anymore to find Jesus. Things improved again as Tim's playground plans went back into their normal emphasis.'

Student take-up

If Jason has had a long weekend with the 'dad', or the de-facto father, he may bring the emotional detritus with him on Monday, thereby making it a more stressful day for both Jason and his teacher. He may reject his behaviour plan and regress on those days. I've had some teachers then say the programme has consequently failed. Not so. On the 'bad days' we need to accept that it is 'bad-day syndrome'. We too, as adults, have bad days. It's just that we are more successful in managing our bad days (generally). While never excusing hostile and aggressive behaviour in the children, teachers can be sensitive to the circumstances that may occasion it.

On those bad days when the child throws his plan on the floor, throws a tantrum, or acts regressively, the teacher needs to still apply the normal classroom discipline procedures and treat the student (respect-fully), as if he's made a choice about his behaviour. Immediate cool-off time and time-out procedures will probably be necessary with follow-up consequences later. The student will start afresh with his plan on return to the classroom — the student's plan is the 'normalising reference point' for the student's behaviour in class.

What we are looking for is approximation to the norm. For some children this takes longer. Like everyone, children learn at different rates, subject to mood and circumstance. When bad-day syndrome is recog-nised, as a common feature of classroom behaviour, the teacher will specifically teach the student ways to enter the class on those days and deal with the 'bad' feelings more productively.

Locus of control

It is important to stress, teach, remind and encourage the student that he is the one who is changing his own behaviour. It is he who is 'making the difference'. Our job is to encourage him to do that; our message to the student is: 'You own your own behaviour — you can make better choices that will see you feeling better as you behave better'. The children's confidence increases as they behave more positively and gain positive peer (and teacher) approval. Success builds confidence and self-esteem.

Behaviour recovery assists locus of control, in students, in the following ways:

- The child learns to manage his own behaviour in a way that *consciously* respects others' rights to feel safe, learn and be treated fairly.
- The child's self-control skills increase so that he no longer relies on the teacher to always mark or check the work ASAP or come immediately when he calls or clicks fingers or shouts (and conversely sulks or whinges). He begins to wait in turn, stay in one place (sit during 'mattime', stay in seat) for a reasonable time.
- Perceptions and beliefs about who really controls (his) behaviour begin to change from others making him behave to choosing to behave as a 'good habit'.
- There is an increase in social skills as the child relates more productively and positively with his peers.

Using self-talk within recovery plans

Cognitive psychologists have long studied the effect of self-talk or self-guiding speech on mood, emotional state and behaviour. The *characteristic* shape and usage of self-talk affects effort, coping behaviour, tolerance to frustration, behavioural outcome and self-esteem (Meichenbaum 1977; Ellis & Bernard 1983; Bernard & Joyce 1984; Braiker 1989; Seligman 1991). The fundamental maxim behind cognitive-behavioural theories is that thinking, emotion and behaviour are inextricably involved with one another. Self-defeating behaviour is related to self-defeating thinking that in turn is related to feeling 'down', unsuccessful and a failure (p. 67).

Demanding assumptions and subsequent self-talk is often couched in imperatives such as 'Teachers *must* be fair'; 'Children *must* like me!'; 'Teachers *shouldn't* tell me what to do'; 'I *hate* maths!'; '*I can't stand* it!'

Such demanding imperatives are characterised by frequency, intensity and generality (they are applied widely and easily). A key feature of pessimistic or demanding self-talk is the lack of re-framing. There is no re-directing, just repeating the same 'explanation'. ('*No one* cares'; '*I always* get things wrong ...') Realistic self-talk adds a qualification. 'OK, I failed, but I don't *always* fail. What can I do to make it better? What can I do to fix it up?'

Cognitive therapists have argued that significant and lasting change includes a change in a person's characteristic thinking patterns. Seligman (1991) has researched the effect of characteristic 'explanatory style' on emotion and functional (or dysfunctional) behaviour. Children can be taught that thinking is a special kind of behaviour. Some thinking makes us feel worse ('I'll *never* be able to do this!'; '*No one* cares about me'; 'I *hate* maths, maths *is* dumb'). Other kinds of thinking will help us to feel better (even when the going gets tough). If students learn to say things like: 'This is hard but if I do my plan it is easier', they will feel better and *do* better. When children (or adults) focus too much on negative or self-defeating explanations they are less likely to feel like exerting the necessary effort to improve things or resolve issues, or even cope.

I recall our four-year-old daughter many years ago talking aloud to herself in the car on a night trip. She was staring at the darkness, the trees flashing past, the waning moon and the quiet night bushscape. In the rear vision mirror I could see (and just hear) her sub-vocalising, 'I'm saying to myself … I'm talking to myself. I'm saying the night might get me a bit nervous'.

Internal conversation is healthy, and the more situation-specific the healthier it's likely to be. For example, characteristic use of global terms like 'Never!'; 'I'm just *too* stupid'; 'No one'; 'Everyone' ('*Everyone* is against me'); 'Can't'; 'Always' ('I *always* muck up'; '*I always* get it wrong') are self-defeating in both mood and behaviour. Children can be taught to re-direct their thinking (as part of their plan) because thinking is a special kind of behaviour that *can be taught*. As Downing (1986) has said: 'By focusing on positive traits and capacities, adults can influence children to relinquish self-defeating behaviours'.

Teaching constructive self-talk

In the one-to-one sessions the teacher can explain (and model) the two kinds of thinking. For example, the teacher models a student's sulky entrance to class, and how the child sulkily flops in his seat, folds his arms and refuses to do the dumb work. While modelling all this she also models

self-talk, aloud: 'Hate this class'; 'Don't care'; 'Work's dumb'; 'Can't do it!'. The student is then asked what might happen if he often says these things upstairs (teacher taps head). The student can be shown a picture of a child thinking negatively or using self-defeating thinking (see PM 13 in the appendix). Again, the balance of teacher modelling, mirroring and picture cues helps to anchor the concepts. The teacher then explains (using a picture cue card) how angry thinking can equal angry behaviour. It is also useful to generalise the issue. 'When we think like *this,* we feel like *this* and we often behave like *this.*' It is important to be specific with the behaviours, thinking and emotion (the feelings).

The next step is to re-frame the desired behaviour within the context of re-framed self-talk. The whole behaviour sequence is repeated and the teacher *says aloud* whichever self-guiding statement is appropriate.

The teacher then models *how* the 'helping thought' can be said quietly 'upstairs', (here teacher taps head) and models the related behaviour. 'Do you know what I just said, Sean?' If the child can't guess, the teacher will explain what just happened in his 'think bubble'. The picture cue card can contain the self-talk as a picture. For children who can read, the self-talk can, of course, be written. The teacher will repeat this several times as per normal rehearsal sessions (see the picture on page 59).

The degree to which the child can comprehend concepts like 'self-talk affecting behaviour' needs to be considered in terms of how much role play is presented regarding self-defeating thinking. Older children can comprehend ideas like, 'When I think I can't do something I often don't even try'; 'When I think I don't care I often feel like it doesn't matter'; 'When I think hopeless, I act hopeless'; 'When I think angry, I ...' With five- to seven-year-olds, it is often appropriate to leave the discussion about negative thoughts and go straight on to teaching positive, self-guiding messages. Teaching 'strong-thinking', 'helpful thoughts' enables the child to focus on this aspect of his *overall* pattern of behaviour while rehearsing the alternative behaviour. The message needs to be simple and directional, often expressed as 'I can ...' or with a 'when/then' statement.

- I can move quickly to my desk, without disturbing others.
- I can sit on my seat without rocking.
- I can speak in a quiet voice.
- I can stay in my seat until the sand runs out on the egg-timer (or whatever timing plan has been developed with the student).
- When I get stuck with my work I can check my work plan again (check with my plan helper, put my hand up to get my teacher).
- When I make a mistake it's OK. I can work out a way to fix it (ask my plan helper or my teacher; see p. 76).

Self-talk can also be practised as affirmations, expressed as if the situation is *actually* happening. Examples include:

- I come to the mat and sit with the others.
- I look at my teacher when she calls my name.
- I share with others.
- I say nice, helpful things to others.
- I walk around the room without disturbing the others.
- I listen when others speak.
- When I get upset I …
- When I get annoyed I …
- When the work is hard I …

Within the reinforcement paradigm the teacher needs to:

- model the self-talk behaviour out aloud ('Sean, watch me. I'm putting my hand up and waiting. Like in our plan I'm saying, 'I can put my hand up without calling out'. You have a go, OK?')
- ask or encourage the child to copy (rehearse)
- model the target behaviour while sub-vocalising
- ask the child to copy the pattern, engaging in his target behaviour *while* sub-vocalising
- check with the child, asking him what was sub-vocalised and encourage him to say this next time in class

Downing (1986) has used taped affirmations that the child listens to several times at certain points during the day. These taped affirmations can be recorded by the teacher and the child, and listened to on headphones. Allied to the picture cue they become a powerful self-reinforcer that in time may become more characteristic of what the child will say in stressful situations.

Encouraging constructive self-talk in classtime

The teacher can often find 'teachable moments in class time' when she can quietly reinforce a child's (potential) positive self-talk. Ben (aged 9) has been taught to develop, and use, his 'partner voice' (for on-task learning time). The grade teacher has also spent some time reinforcing this recovery plan with a 'self-talk' component.

Back in the classroom she notices Ben working at his table group *and* using his partner voice. She walks across and quietly pats his arm and quietly says, 'I bet I know what you were saying in your head …' Ben grins back — even if he wasn't using the self-talk component, the reinforcement acts as a reminder and encourager.

The imaginary helper

With older primary age students the teacher can introduce the student to an imaginary helper (see Wragg 1989). The child is talked through the behavioural tasks. 'You can ... when ...'; 'That's it, you remembered — four-on-the-floor! That's it, it's easier to write when I'm not rocking in my chair!'; 'Yep, put my hand up to get the teacher over here without calling out.'

The teacher explains that in class there will be a helper sitting with him, 'like I've shown you now'. All the time remind him of his plan. The child will laugh, thinking this is a joke. The teacher can even have an empty chair next to the child to simulate this.

T: 'You know who the helper is?'

S: 'No, who?'

T: '*You! You* can be your own helper.'

Here the teacher can explain how thinking helps (or hinders) behaviour. She can first model the self-talk strategy with the students and then rehearse it.

It can be explained to older children that sometimes people forget (upstairs in our thinking) and say really unhelpful things to themselves. When they catch themselves saying these things they need to stop and remember their plan. 'Thought-stopping' can become a positive habit. 'I really stuffed that one up! I'm really stupid! Hang on, Bill (the thought-stopper) it's OK to make mistakes; mistakes don't make me stupid. What can I do to fix things up?' Thought-stoppers (Braiker 1989; Seligman 1991) put a check on the *negative run of thinking* so the thought can be recognised and *re-framed*.

Thought-stopping reminders can be put on to a small card with a catchy heading. 'Catch me thinking'; 'When I'm in control I say ...'; 'Helpful thoughts equal helpful behaviour.' The students can have several helpful thoughts to remember when under pressure in the classroom. 'Take it easy mate'; 'Hang in there'; 'You can do it'; 'Count to ten'; 'Take four deep breaths' (Wragg 1989).

One student (Year 5) I worked with had problems with attention and restlessness. He'd constantly turn around to annoy others and was off-task frequently. The cue card had a picture of him head down with a talk/think bubble saying, 'Hang in there! You can do it!' We'd rehearsed that he had 'to go', head down, working away until I came over to touch him on the shoulder. I set my watch timer for three minutes and came over every three minutes when it 'beeped' to *briefly* encourage him. He did almost ten minutes of the language task set (which for this student was a significant change in behaviour). The card sat on his desk, with the thought cue, alongside his work. He was being encouraged to be 'his own helper' with support from me. The time lapses increased from two to five to ten minutes (see PM 17c in the appendix, and p. 74).

Behaviour teaching cards: a case study

... (behaviour recovery teaching) cards are a fabulous and innovative method for modifying behaviour. I have been able to use these recovery teaching cards quickly and successfully with a variety of behaviour problems. Teachers monitoring the cards have commented on the ease of implementing the programme, and have also commended the card's illustrations, which clearly show the target behaviour. The children's responses to the cards have been totally enthusiastic, particularly the pictorial presentation and the in-built reward/merit system.

I feel that recovery-teaching cards are particularly effective as they clearly show peer responses to the inappropriate and appropriate behaviour being exhibited by the child. The picture cues (the card) are also helpful, visual reminders. They are effective in reinforcing the desired behaviour. The cards may be used effectively in conjunction with learning difficulties and programmes to encourage children to read and write. They complement on-task training with their visual representation of which behaviour is on-task.

Caroline: behaviour management teacher

Motivating Students with Emotional Behavioural Disorder 4

Children with behaviour disorders often experience some rejection by their peers and (at times) weary teachers who may not mean to reject them. Teachers may become disillusioned and discouraged at the student's apparent failure to respond to classroom management and learning programmes. These students may present as having poor incentive with limited effort. Frequently described as socially disruptive, the disruptive behaviour may itself (Dreikurs 1968, Dreikurs et al. 1982) be the child's unfortunate (if annoying) attempt to find a social place — a 'compensating' social place; that is, his misguided — disruptively misguided — attempt at 'belonging' with his school-age peers (p. 50).

The importance of motivation

Teachers use motivation in both internal and external ways in an effort to stimulate the student to positive action. Both will be needed, both overlap. Of course, the ideal is (as is the goal of any behaviour enhancement programme) to increase the student's locus of control so that he:

- is not *everly reliant* on teacher direction and encouragement alone; that he can control his *own* behaviour
- *consciously* respects others' rights
- has skills of social interaction and on-task behaviour that don't rely on constant reminders or intervention by the teacher
- perceives that he really can control his behaviour and direct his rational world.

Rehearsal time and in-class encouragement and feedback are directed to these motivational goals.

One of the important goals of behaviour recovery is to strengthen the student's belief in his ability to relate socially — in positive ways. These ways need to be taught.

The teaching cards in the Behaviour Recovery programme depict social approval and social disapproval. These teaching cards are themselves visual reminders of the *process* of the child's plan and can be used to motivate the student towards social approval.

If the class teacher (or tutor) has classroom meeting feedback (see Chapter 5) this too can be used to challenge the child towards the positive behaviours within each recovery plan. The classroom meeting feedback should only concentrate on what his fellow students *fairly* want him to do. Negative behaviours can be added as an 'instead of'. 'Your classmates want you to put your hand up instead of calling out.' 'Your classmates want you to (be specific) instead of ... (be specific).' It is also important to remind the class members to encourage positive behaviour and support one another's co-operative efforts (see classroom meetings Chapter 5).

During rehearsal (practice) and class time the teacher can use phrases like, 'You can do it!'; 'Hang in there, you'll get it'; 'It might be hard (the work) but keep trying'. Encourager cards can help to develop frustration tolerance. These cards can sit on the desk with the encouraging words with pictures included in the picture cues. Plan helpers (see pp. 76 and 78) are also a source of motivation.

Motivation and self-esteem are powerfully linked. As the teacher and his peers begin to value the child, behavioural success enhances his value (esteem) of himself. Extrinsic esteem increases self-esteem. If the student participates in self-esteem programmes that are part of the classroom curriculum for all students, there will be significant overlap with the messages he is receiving in recovery time. Class teachers (in most cases) are 'significant others' in the lives of students. The special one-to-one time that behaviour recovery allows is itself a powerful extrinsic motivator.

'Rewards' as behaviour encouragement

Each recovery plan that forms part of the recovery process can be linked to extrinsic rewards. At the bottom of each card are 'boxes' that can be ticked off, or shaded in, several times a day on direction from the teacher. Each ticked or shaded box signifies an occasion when the student has kept to his plan. Many teachers use these extrinsic motivators to 'kick-start' the success needed for students. When all the boxes are ticked or shaded, the student can trade in his effort for a 'reward' (free-time activity, stamps/stickers, voucher at the canteen, or even a whole-class reward. As each card is filled in (for each set of behaviours) the prompting should fade, the number of boxes be increased — or shaded in after several (rather than individual) occurrences of the on-task behaviour.

I've put inverted commas around the word reward. I prefer the word 'celebration' rather than reward when talking with the child. It is important to get away from ideas of 'earning' rewards or *any* hint of 'bribing' the student; 'if you do this ... and get all these ticks ... then you'll get a reward!'

Rather 'when the boxes are all ticked we'll celebrate with ...' As with any 'intervention' programme designed to build some extrinsic motivation into a child's effort, and progress, it is always worth discussing extrinsic motivation approaches with colleagues.

When planning 'academic' work for students on recovery programmes it is important to discuss with the special needs teacher how best to pitch the work for likely success. The way the work is set out and scheduled is important to consequent success in behaviour recovery. Workplans, with the set tasks broken down into achievable timeslots, help keep the potential for success achievable.

The most important motivator is the teacher and her belief in the child. Of course, these children weary teachers. Of course, teachers get frustrated (even exasperated at times) — that's natural. However, if they repair and rebuild each day, the message, 'I believe you can do it', is likely to get through.

Failure

It is really important that the teacher spend a little time encouraging the child to be 'allowed to fail'. Even some adults find the concept and feelings associated with failure difficult at times. Even momentary failure can occasion the feeling of an emotional kick in the stomach. 'How could I be so stupid!?' Failure also sees some people *rating* themselves against others' typical successful behaviour.

It is crucial that the child *learns* to distinguish between failure and *being* a failure. When our 'characteristic explanatory style' is to *over-rate* before unpleasant events or experiences, our self-explanation can have as much an effect on our negative feelings as the *fact* that we did fail in a given instance (Seligman 1991). We cannot *be* a failure, though we do *naturally and normally* fail in given instances. Some people use failure *experiences* as proof that 'I *always fail*', 'I'll *never get it right*', through to 'I *can't* do this ...', 'I'll *never* be able to do this' and '*This will last forever ...*'

While it *is* unpleasant when we fail, or struggle hard and have set-backs when learning *anything* new, that failure is mostly normal and natural to the learning process. While not denying the jaded feelings we get when we fail, it is important to learn to recognise that:

- 'yes I did fail, didn't get it right' (it is important not to *deny* that we failed)
- failure is OK, normal to learning (even if the feelings are sometimes unpleasant)
- there is a big difference between failing (momentarily) and using our self-talk to punish ourselves *as if we are a failure*
- *failure and practice go together.*

Whenever my colleagues and I work with a student on new behaviour or 'academic learning' skills, we emphasise the analogy of practice. This includes focusing on a skill the child has already mastered, such as 'game-boy', computer games, football, swimming, callisthenics and so on. We then discuss the *practice principle*; for example, how we felt the first time we hopped into a pool. 'Could we swim *well*' or 'kick a footy *well*, 'master the computer game' ... the first time, the first few times? What made it better?

- We *wanted* to learn.
- We had *someone help us* with the skill we wanted or needed.
- We *practised.* We put in the effort. Even a 'minimum' amount of effort will help change motivation and, further, help in positive responses from teacher and peers. Here is a reminder card on 'time' (with a Grade 5 student); the numbers are minutes of 'practice'.

Figure 4.1 Minutes of my plan

	am	pm
Monday	10, 15, 20	10, 15, 20
Tuesday	10, 15, 20	10, 15, 20
Wednesday	10, 15, 20	10, 15, 20
Thursday	10, 15, 20	10, 15, 20
Friday	10, 15, 20	10, 15, 20
	= Lots!	= Lots!

A minimum amount of effort; it will change things, bit by bit

- We failed and we *learned from our failure*. I can remember when ... often I've appropriately shared with children times I've failed in learning new things. When a teacher 'normalises' failure — as part of the learning cycle — it will assist the supportive nature of the recovery approach.
- We didn't criticise ourselves (too much we hope) when we failed.

That is how we, as adults, learned to drive. I can recall the anxious first lessons of driving a ute through a fence! I also remember some anxious moments teaching my daughter to drive. She's fine now.

It is crucial that in the natural setting of the classroom any teacher — or assistant teacher — be alert to a child's over-focusing on failure and use *quiet,* quick, 'private' and encouraging reminders about keeping on with the plan.

The effects of failure

Of course, failure is meaningful only if we actually learn from it! This, too, is a positive habit to develop — *failing meaningfully*.

- Knowing what behaviours are ineffective or inappropriate (even the way a child organises, or 'disorganises', his work area).
- Knowing the self-talk we use when we fail. Learning to tune-in to our self-talk can be a useful habit, so that we can re-frame such self-talk when it moves into self-defeating generalisation: 'I *shouldn't* have!' (I did); 'I am an idiot!' (played over and over); 'I *never* ...'; 'I *just can't*'; 'It's just *too* hard ...' (see p. 57).

> Children are so familiar with the concept of CDs my colleagues and I have used the kinaesthetic image of writing a new 'CD' to 'play upstairs'. This 'CD' can be a small disc with the new, improved 'self-talk' written on. This is laminated and becomes a personal, 'iconic', *aide memoir*.

Supportive feedback

Use the support of a teacher or classmate to:

- learn about what to do next time
- refine your plan, keep the *practice* going
- learn to recognise success, and acknowledge and affirm the progress of the skill. 'You did it ... you organised the workplace quickly'; 'You read through, carefully, what you had to do in your work ...'; 'You asked

the right questions ('What am I asked to do now…'); you didn't rush it …' 'You dated the work and got half the set work done. Well done!'

Teacher expectations

Teacher attitude and expectations are constantly conveyed and picked up by students in the following ways:

- The *kind* of attention given. It is easier to attend to 'brighter', 'self-motivated' students. Teachers may tend to call on the 'brighter' students to the exclusion of others (especially distracting and attentional students). This is exacerbated *because* such students often demand attention in disruptive ways (hence, the need for a *structured* approach to help them develop positive behaviours).
- The way we address mistakes or failures. It is easier to accept mistakes or failure in 'brighter' children than to accept that the children with special needs and behaviour disorders actually made a mistake.
- The way in which tasks are set; for example, he'd *never* be able to do that.
- The way we engage in class discussion. Calling on students in class to contribute may mean, in fact, only expecting certain students to be able to contribute productively. This is where classroom meetings can be valuable in helping all children to believe that their contribution is useful (see Chapter 5).

I once observed a teacher admonish a young student during quiet reading time because he had chosen an encyclopaedia to read. Worse, she did it publicly. In tone and gesture she effectively put him down in the very area in which she needed to build him up. Teacher expectations can be communicated through the appalling labels that some teachers give to children's behaviour, such as 'stupid', 'dumb', 'twit', 'dropkick' or the over-generalisations, such as 'You *always* …'; You *never* …'; '*Can't* you … ?'; 'You *can't* …'; You *should* be able to do that by now …'

It is important to acknowledge basics such as using the child's first name, knowing his interests and speaking to him (acknowledging him) out of class (Rogers 1998).

As noted earlier most encouragement can be given briefly, even non-verbally. Wheldhall (1991) has noted that the use of 'contingent-touch' when praising (lower primary) children for 'appropriate academic and/or social behaviour', saw an increase in on-task behaviour by over 15 per cent in some classroom trials (pp. 57–9). I have also noticed that the thoughtful, considered use of 'directional-touch' increased behavioural outcomes and more positive teacher–student rapport.

For example, when reminding students to pack up, the teacher can come side-on to the lazier students and say, 'David, I want you to put the unifix blocks away now, then you can do your writing'. As she says this, she looks towards the blocks and points. She pats him on the arm a couple of times and leaves with a beckoning hand directing to the blocks. If he whines or argues ('But Angelo didn't put his blocks away!') the teacher will *redirect*. 'I'll speak to Angelo, I want you to put the blocks away now, thanks.' The teacher pats his arm and walks slowly away, giving him 'take-up-time' (Rogers 1998). If he refuses to pack up the teacher will clarify the consequence. When he does as required she can briefly acknowledge him, even with a directional OK sign across the room. If the teacher is spatially close she can pat him on the arm, with a brief 'thanks'.

This kind of encouragement doesn't take long. It is the teacher's conscious and characteristic awareness about her behaviour *in relationship* to the child that will often make the difference.

Encouragement

Encouragement enables the child to develop his strengths. It gives him the courage to 'fail' and learn from failure, or to 'grow'. It can be as basic as a wink, smile, touch on the arm, the 'good-on-you' sign (thumbs up or the 'OK' signal) or the *descriptive* feedback the teacher gives about tasks, learning or behaviour.

Damien: a case study

I was conducting a lesson on process writing (using the children's favourite authors as a framework for what makes any kind of writing interesting or, even, exciting). Several teachers had come to observe the lesson. During the on-task phase, I moved around the room, encouraging, giving feedback, and a little corrective discipline here and there.

The most troublesome student was sitting by himself (as part of the regular class teacher's discipline plan) — the requirement was that he work in isolation.

On walking over to Damien ('How's it going Damien?') I noticed he had written a great deal. 'Messily' — yes, and with 'missing' punctuation, but positive effort had been applied. I asked him if I could have a read. ('Yeah — course!') He had written a story with thoughtful characters and a workable plot line. He was clearly enthused by what he had done. 'You've written heaps, and you're still not finished Damien'. I commented on his characters and plot adding, 'Well done, hang in there'. I thought I'd call his teacher over to have a look (she was sitting at the back of the room observing). She came over and I showed her Damien's effort. She looked at it (without asking before she picked it up) and said, 'Yes, Mr Rogers, but did you notice how messy the writing is?' It wasn't just her pursed lips, her controlled 'Snappy-Tom' voice, it was the focus: she totally missed the effort Damien had given to his work.

Some teachers believe that if they *don't* criticise then nothing will change or get done. The purpose of encouragement lies not in false praise ('Good boy', 'Good girl') but in focusing, and helping the student to focus, on the effort given or required for a task. It is important to use descriptive feedback rather than *mere* criticism. Children need to know where they are going wrong (or if they are not achieving a target). This is best done quietly, without unnecessary embarrassment and in some cases it is most effective on a one-to-one basis. Students can be taught to self-correct daily and in recovery (one-to-one) sessions using questions such as these:

- What was the easiest part of your plan today (or this week) and why?
- What was the hardest part and why?
- What do you feel when ...? (Be specific.)
- Can you remember what you did when ... ? (Help the student to recall both positive and negative behaviours.) Mirroring can help here.
- What can you do instead of ...? (Be *specific* about the incorrect behaviours.)
- What can you do *next* time? (Be specific.)

Verbal encouragement

The hardest part about any encouragement is remembering to give it and getting used to 'looking' for opportunities to even *briefly* encourage. One noticeable aspect of the encouragement used in rehearsal sessions with students is that it may spill over into *normative* encouragement by the teacher during in-class time.

- 'You did a good job of ...' (Be specific.)
- 'Thanks for working *quietly* (or helpfully, politely, carefully).
- 'Thanks for waiting while I was busy with ...'
- 'I liked the way you remembered to walk quietly to your desk.'
- 'Good manners there.'
- 'If you keep smiling like that (or helping like that), people will be happy because ... Do you know what will happen if you keep ...? (mention their positive behaviour) They'll be happy!' (p. 121)
- 'Good on you for ...?' (Here specify what.)
- 'You remembered your plan to ... Well done.' (Be specific.)

A colleague of mine had a student who improved through his plan by the teacher's use of peer encouragement and telegraphing expectation. She pre-arranged with several students (in class) to use positive reminders to the student (on the plan). For example, Matthew (the child on the plan) would approach their table or borrow their equipment. They were encouraged to respond with phrases like 'Hi, Matthew, want to borrow a texta?' This gave Matthew a chance to ask appropriately. The teacher also backed this up with 'test runs' (similar to the rehearsed behaviours). 'Matthew, I want you to go to Paul and Lisa's table and ...' (Here she specified a positive social behaviour task.) The students would then give some brief positive encouragement to Matthew based on the classroom meeting suggestions on how to encourage one another (see p. 89).

As Rosenthal and Jacobsen (1967) have shown, shortcomings in academic performance and social behaviour are not merely explained by the fact that the child is a member of a disadvantaged group. 'There may well be another reason. It is that the child who does poorly in school because that is what is expected of him. In other words, his shortcomings may originate not in his different ethnic, cultural and economic background, but in his teacher's response to that background' (p. 184). Rosenthal and Jacobsen have also conducted a number of experiments that highlighted what all teachers know (in their more reflective moments) that expectation does affect outcomes. (See Silberman 1970 and Rogers forthcoming.)

Rosenthal and Jacobsen randomly selected students who were allocated to teachers with descriptors such as 'spurters' and 'slow track'. The experimental treatment focused on labelling students as children who could be *expected* to perform well or poorly. The difference between the groups was 'entirely in the minds of the teachers'. What is intriguing is that the children, 'from whom intellectual growth was expected were described as having a better chance at being successful in later life and being happier, more curious and more interesting than the other children'.

I have noticed a similar phenomenon with behaviour and expectation. Rosenthal and Jacobsen explain that this expectation probably lies in the subtler features of the interaction of the teacher and her pupils, such as tone of voice, facial expressions, touch and posture. This 'may be the means by which — probably quite unwittingly — she communicates her expectations to the pupils. Such communication might help the child by changing his conception of himself, his anticipation of his own behaviour, his motivation or his cognitive skills' (p. 188). Teachers will admit, though, having to work against their feelings at times ('I *feel* he won't do well'; 'He *always* calls out ...'; 'He *never* finishes his work') and remembering to encourage when it is appropriate. Not an easy task but a necessary one.

Older children, ADD and task focus

My colleagues and I have found that there are a number of skills that can give some focus, direction, motivation and confidence to children when it comes to directing themselves to a learning task and developing *habits* of concentration and effort when engaged in such activities.

Many of the children we have worked with have a negative attitude to their learning; to the expectations of pressure that school can be for some children. Some are quite anxious about 'success' and not meeting their perceptions of peer (or teacher or parent) success. This anxiety can manifest itself in attentional/avoidance behaviours. Some children can become quite 'expert' at task-avoidance. In its mild to extreme forms, task-avoidance may be for many children a way of protecting their self-esteem — when only mistakes and failure are the 'normal expectation' of self and others. These children may have developed habits of *thinking* and behaviour that filter out positive learning experiences of the past, leading them to avoidance behaviours in the present ('Well if I'm no good at ... and I don't do it ... I won't fail ...'). By *not* doing something (for example, a learning task) they don't feel *as* bad — because at least they are not failing.

Our role, in behaviour recovery, is to encourage the child to learn the *skills* that will enable him to think and (bit by bit) behave as an effective learner. 'Also, if you behave differently you'll find it could change how your classmates, teachers or parents get on with you. Also, you'll feel better about school and what we're learning together. A minimum amount of effort is required and you'll see it will add up.' (See page 68.)

The emphasis (one-to-one) with the student will be to encourage him to see the purpose of these skills:

- These skills will help him with his *everyday* learning; no matter the task.
- Skills in learning are like skills in anything ('football', 'basketball', 'swimming', 'knitting' or 'playing an instrument') — they require *practice* (p. 68). Behaviour recovery puts a great deal of emphasis on practice through supportive *behaviour rehearsal* and feedback (pp. 43–8).

Key skills in developing focus and attention

Children 'with' ADDH are sometimes forgetful, disorganised and easily distracted. In instructional/teaching time they may be inattentive (for example, turning around and eye-balling other students; heavy seat rocking; slumping down over the table; chatting while the teacher is talking or leading a discussion). If this is the typical behaviour of the child, the teacher can 'mirror' those behaviours and explain, identify and model the new listening and concentration behaviours, for example, such as *facing the front* and *looking* at the board/teacher/presentation; *listening* to the teaching/or class discussion by *looking* and ...; joining in class discussions fairly ('hands up without calling out'); *waiting one's turn*; *listening to fellow students*; and not talking over them.

When a student moves from 'instructional' to 'on-task' time it will be important to have rehearsed the importance of 'advance organisers' within their time-on-task plan (their 'learning plan'). As with any behaviour recovery plan the teacher will identify and explain what the skills are (and why the student needs them), use role-modelling ('mirroring' and modelling), use rehearsal and feedback, and explain how the plan will be used in the classroom (see Chapter 3).

Advance organisers

The student can have a simple reminder list to help him 'get started' on his 'subject' task for *that* lesson. At infant-age level, teachers often use a small card with the child's photo on it and key words (or logos) to remind him what to do. Some children will benefit from a different card for each key learning area that day. It will also be important to model (one-to-one) and rehearse what a reasonably organised desk looks like. Never assume.

At upper primary level, a standard card (with or without photo) with several key reminders for task-learning time is required. It should contain directives such as:

1 Organise your desk space (as we practised).

2 Organise your pencil case.

3 Check for the right work book.

4 Read through the *bbw* (book, board, worksheet).

5 What am I asked to do now? (check *bbw*)

6 Ask for teacher help if you need it. Remember our class rule. (It is important that the child remembers the class rule or routine for asking teacher help or conference time. Routines vary widely among classes.)

7 Check your margin and date. Well done _____ (name of child).

Many teachers in upper primary (middle school) encourage their children to colour-code their work books. This simple colour-code (for example, yellow cover — English) can go on the back of their learning reminder card.

Table pencil case

I have worked with many children who often have a pencil case that needs a crane to get it on their table! It is full of tempting and time-wasting *objets d'art* (old mini-skateboards, small toys, felt-tip pens that don't work, broken pens, string, old sandwiches).

We *strongly* suggest they put this pencil case in 'the garage' (locker) and use a *table pencil case* (small) with one red and blue pen, one pencil, an eraser, a 15 cm ruler and no sharpener.

It also helps to quietly and privately encourage the child while at his desk/table (once he has started the task — even minimally) with his plan. Use the following strategies:

- 'You started quickly Jason — see your table pencil case there ...'
- 'What do you have to do *now?* Check your card.' (Visual prompt to card — p. 75.)

It can also help to encourage them to go over the task instructions for that activity: *'Read through ... What am I asked to do? How will I start? Off we go ... now'*. It will always help to break up larger tasks into smaller ones. One student (Cain) I worked with some years back started off with five-minute task time segments built up to fifteen minutes task segments over a term. After each five minutes the teacher would go over to rein-force, encourage and give feedback.

Some students will get excited about their new plan and may rush to complete a learning task (particularly if the teacher has a 'reward system' linked to a child's learning plan). The student will need to learn some basic quality checks for their work, not just quantity. This aspect of his plan also needs to be clearly discussed in one-to-one time.

Pack-up routines

To keep some habituated organisational focus it will help if the student has a standard pack-up and basic tidy routine for his desk or locker, so he doesn't get discouraged when the locker is a mess of jumbled papers and odd and ends — spot checks and positive reinforcement will help.

Enlisting the support of a 'plan helper'

One way to consolidate, and encourage, positive behaviour is by teaming the student (on a recovery plan) with one of his peers — giving him, in effect, a plan helper. The class teacher selects a few likely and willing can-didates (those with common sense and positive social skills) and asks them if they would like to help their classmate with his plan. This role can also be taken on by a student from another class who comes in to do cross-age tutoring (within the plan). Ideally, the plan-helper is a fellow student who can sit near him each day. The role of plan helper can be rotated over several weeks if necessary. It is a surprise to some teachers just how responsible and supportive students can be in this role. The 'plan helper's' job description is to help their fellow student with his plan; not to do it for him (their role is to remind, encourage and help).

Chris and his plan-helper (infants)

Part of Chris's behaviour recovery plan involved going to his class locker before each writing activity or maths task to get his egg-timer. He used the egg-timer (in three- to five-minute bursts) to focus on his task without seat-rocking, seat-wandering or turning around. He sat the egg-timer on his desk, worked for three minutes, ticked a 'finished-a-bit-box', and then put his hand up. The teacher then came over for a brief bit of encouragement, or gave 'private cues' across the room (see p. 48). With the assistance of a plan helper the teacher's role — to remind and encourage — was enhanced. The plan helper reminded Chris if he forgot to get his egg-timer, to sit four-on-the-floor, and to put his hand up without calling out. He even used some of the privately understood signals (as used by the teacher).

Teachers can brief the plan helper with some helpful cue phrases for reminding and encouraging. When the student (who is on a recovery plan) 'forgets', 'wanders' or 'rocks', the plan helper can quietly act as teacher support. The other advantage of such support is the increase in peer-group interaction; especially when the child is encouraged by a peer for doing the right thing.

The role of plan helper is also beneficial in the development of social supportive skills and is at the heart of co-operative learning. The child on such a plan will need to feel that he wants the help of a classmate so he is offered three names from which to choose. 'Which of these three students would you like to help you with your plan?' The plan helper can even sit in on some of the recovery sessions (the one-to-one sessions) to get an idea of the target behaviours (if their classmate is willing). It is explained to the child that 'x' is going to 'help you with your plan in class'. The child should be asked where he would like his plan helper to sit.

Peer encouragement

Van Houten (1980) notes a number of studies which demonstrate that, while children frequently reinforce, or attend, to misbehaviour in their peers, they can also be taught to attend to positive behaviours. Key students were selected as 'peer therapists' or 'peer encouragers'. They were then taught how they could help reduce disruptive behaviour and increase the occurrence of more appropriate classroom behaviour.

After being trained to spot instances of on-task attention and desirable behaviour, they were given instruction on how they could encourage and attend to those behaviours and what behaviours they could 'ignore'. They (the peer therapists) also learned to keep daily records, which they discussed with their teacher at the close of each day. The studies showed that peers could (by their conscious intervention) influence the behaviours of fellow disruptive students.

It is worth noting that this role (of 'plan helper') may cause concern in *some* parents — that their child is being asked 'to work with a naughty child' and that this is unfair — drawing them away from valuable classroom learning time. In fact, there is valuable 'classroom learning' taking place. The plan helper is developing social skills of empathy, supportive common sense and perspective-taking. This role can be rotated weekly (with several students) in the establishment phase of a student's recovery plan.

It is important that the role of plan helper is voluntary and the student has a positive working relationship with the student 'on a plan'.

Utilising the Child's Peers to Support Behaviour Recovery 5

When a child comes into a naturally socially demanding context like school a prime motivation for behaviour will be social belonging; whatever his 'emotional pathology'. The child, in effect, asks 'How do I belong here? How do I gain a place of significance, purpose and power? How do I fit in?' (Dreikurs 1968, 1985). While many children (fortunately for general sanity!) find constructive ways to belong, a small percentage seek counter-productive ways to gain social credibility. This is a crucial understanding when considering repeatedly distracting and disruptive behaviours of an individual *within a group context*.

When a child repeatedly (and annoyingly) calls out, whines, wanders, butts in, won't sit on the mat during mat-time, won't line-up, join in or do his work, he is not merely trying to gain attention or provoke a power exchange. He is often seeking to 'belong' *through* those behaviours. Within his own selective frame of reference he believes that these behaviours gain him a 'place' and, of course, when teachers and fellow students, over-service (over-attend or 'buy-into') those behaviours the child's mistaken belief is confirmed.

The class giggles among themselves when Jason is under the table and his teacher is raising her voice to get him out, or pleads with him to come out or drags him out kicking and screaming. The class giggling reinforces the child's selective and mistaken belief about 'how to belong'. If the child regularly refuses to do the work (assuming he is able to do it), or refuses to join in, or pack up and the teacher argues and verbally fights back and threatens (often with the work still not being done) the child believes he is powerful in this exchange. This 'belief' may be internalised as, 'I can do what I want and no one can stop me ...'; 'I can do what I want, when I want; I'm the boss I'm in charge!' (pp. 50–1). These children are often alienated from their peers, laughed at or over-serviced by them when they are acting disruptively. The long-term outcome of behaviour recovery is to enable the child to belong (and gain peer acceptance) using considerate, positive or social behaviours.

Behaviour recovery utilises one-to-one attention in order to develop purposeful belonging by drawing constructive attention to peer approval and peer disapproval. Utilising the child's desire to belong, the teacher can use rehearsal sessions to motivate that desire.

Classroom meetings

The personal satisfaction of a *positive* peer acceptance, of doing the right thing and of *belonging in a worthwhile way* is a central goal of all classroom management (and of behaviour recovery in particular). The teacher can reinforce this by using classroom meetings to enlist whole-class support for the student on a recovery plan. Further support can be garnered using peer helpers (see Chapter 4).

Classroom meetings are a well-established feature of classroom life in many primary schools (Nelson 1981; Rogers 1998 and 2003; Dempster & Raff 1992). Many primary schools use classroom meetings on a regular basis to allow students to open up a topic, explore a range of options, share opinions, think aloud, hear what others value, believe in, and feel about common concerns within a common forum. The meetings can be used to discuss an educational topic in a general or focused way. They can also be used to assess a topic, plan a programme or evaluate classroom life. For example, at the end of each term it is worth asking the questions, 'What has worked well in our class (for you, for us all) this term and why?'; 'What hasn't worked well and why?'; 'What can we do to improve things or make them better?' If children are given genuine opportunity to share their ideas, test out opinions, share concerns and look for solutions — they are then valued. They can believe that they are given the dignity of involvement and participation in classroom life. They will come to believe that they and their concerns, ideas and opinions count.

If classroom meetings are used as a regular forum, an agenda board can list topics for discussion by individuals, or the teacher. In fact, many concerns of individuals can be dealt with in this way by asking the child, 'Do you want to raise this in meeting time? Do you want to have it noted on the board?' This, of course, should be carried out only with the child's willing co-operation. Regular use of classroom meetings helps satisfy the

social needs of belonging and participation, where self-concept can be strengthened, problem-solving skills enhanced, and a challenging and enjoyable forum for healthy discussion provided.

In terms of supporting students, the kind of classroom meeting discussed here is a problem-solving meeting. Such a meeting provides a number of opportunities:

- A forum for raising an issue of common concern to both teacher and students (for example, teasing, fighting, 'tale-telling', bullying, swearing or put-downs).
- An outlet of concern for all students. They all hear the same things, the concerns, the opinions, how people feel, what suggestions are made, what the outcome will be.
- A forum for enlisting class support (with the teacher) for working with a student who is on a recovery plan.
- Shared outcomes agreed to by all the students.

Such a meeting can also address issues affecting classroom learning, such as repeated calling out/butting in, students who talk while the teacher is teaching and inappropriate noise (levels) in on-task learning time.

Any outcome decided through classroom meetings (particularly, a consequence) needs to be assessed within the normal test of:

- Is it *fair and reasonable* (by our classroom rights and rules)?
- Is the consequence, or outcome, *related* to the issue or behaviour we are discussing?
- Can we actually carry it out?
- Most of all, does the outcome we decide *keep the respect* (of the individual and group) intact?

If these conditions are not met the outcome/consequence is not pursued. When discussing consequences for behaviours like swearing, aggression and bullying, some children can be quite Draconian. Students need to reflect on the difference between a consequence and 'pay-back' or revenge! One way of emphasising this is to ask if this consequence will really or actually help teach the students to change their behaviour.

One of my colleagues has a sign (on his Year 6 classroom wall), referred to during all classroom meetings: *'Is it related? Is it reasonable? Does it keep respect intact? If it doesn't we don't use it.'*

Planning a meeting

A specific time and topic is set aside by the teacher, telegraphed early to the class: 'On Wednesday we'll be having a special classroom meeting to discuss ...' The topic could be in-class concerns raised by the students (or teacher), or it could focus on an individual's behaviour in particular.

The seating should be arranged in a circle to enhance visual and auditory communication. If the desks are all facing the same way (that is, the front of the room) it is often difficult for everyone to hear. The circle plan allows everybody to see and hear everyone else. It is important for the teacher to sit at the same level, whether on chairs or on the floor. Plan ahead how the chairs can be moved into a circle and the desks to the side. Brainstorm suggestions from the class group and pick the best so there is a routine for all classroom meetings.

It is essential to develop some rules for the meeting. While the rules for a classroom meeting are similar to normal classroom rules, the *focus* of the relevant classroom rules will need to be made clear.

Communication: listen and look when someone is sharing. Give others a fair go. Check with someone if you don't understand what they mean. Often it will be the teacher who facilitates clarification by feedback and active listening. In this the teacher provides a model for the students. For the garrulous set a limit of three turns so that they do not dominate. Dempster and Raff (1992) suggest a novel approach. Each person has several counters or blocks, each one representing a contribution to the discussion. These are placed in the centre of the circle as each contribution is made. Once they've used up all their blocks, they're 'out'. A fair routine.

Treatment: this is the crucial rule. We talk about behaviour; we don't attack people or their ideas. We don't put people down. (This aspect of the rule is crucial to enforce, especially when discussing individual students and their behaviour.) We use positive language.

Safety: keep your hands and feet to yourself.

Decisions: we decide together. The group, and the individuals, have to accept the group's decision.

Classroom meetings are sometimes called 'magic circles' or 'circle times' (in infant and primary years). Here is an example of the rules used in one school for 'magic circle' time.

- Look and listen.
- Only bring yourself to the mat (no toys, or distracting objects).
- What is said in the circle stays in the circle. (This is an ambitious rule.)
- Respect other people's ideas and opinions.

These rules were published on a large disc of coloured card and laminated. They remained in the room and were referred to as necessary. Listening skills were practised in small groups of three to six children to enhance the quality of listening in 'magic circle time'. The basic skills (for use in meeting times) were published on a large card with cartoons (laminated) and referred to by the teacher and the group when necessary: *face the person; look at the person; listen with your ears; lean forward; keep still; active listening — repeat back what you heard; say what you think is meant and check to see if you're right.*

Conducting a meeting

It is the tone set by the teacher that largely determines the success of classroom meetings. Dominating the meeting by disagreeing with suggestions or ideas or, worse, putting them down, works against the very purpose for which the meeting has been planned. It is important that the teacher creates and sustains a caring and open environment where students have a genuine opportunity to have their say, express themselves, make suggestions and participate in decisions within fair guidelines. If teachers merely use classroom meeting times to dominate the agenda and force a predetermined decision, students will quickly realise this and merely acquiesce or submit to what they think the teacher wants.

If meetings are held on a regular basis it can be useful to build in a positive sharing time for the class group. Students are invited to share positive outcomes from the week, either general or directed to another student. Teachers often need to give several examples to start with (keeping a notebook helps because it is easy to forget the positive behaviours and outcomes of a busy week) (Nelson 1981; Dempster & Raff 1992). Specific positives or 'encouragers' are important (not merely 'I like David'). 'I liked it when Jason ...'; 'I was helped by ... Thanks'; 'I noticed the way Paul and Maria helped out by ... Thanks'; 'That was a great game, wasn't it? I appreciated the fair play of ...'

Conducting a classroom meeting is not easy. We have to keep the focus, facilitate, draw out the more hesitant, check for understanding by giving feedback and use active listening ('Do you mean?'; 'Are you saying?') The teacher needs to avoid easy judgement yet clarify possible outcomes of what is being said. 'What would happen if we did, or said, that?'; 'How does that fit in with our classroom rules?'; 'Does that solution fit our test of a helpful solution?' (Is it fair? Does it relate to the problem or the behaviour itself? What will the person learn if the class does that? Does it show respect? (p. 82))

Discipline during the meeting should follow the conventions of normal classroom discipline (see Chapter 6). Students can be reminded or directed towards the desired behaviour. Sometimes this can be done with a non-verbal signal. If a student persists in butting in, or seat-hopping, or using put-downs, he should be warned to follow the rules for the meeting or sit out (time-out outside the circle).

This needs to be enforced for the benefit of everyone in the class group. If the student will not sit out, the supported exit provision can be used (see p. 109) and the student followed up later by the classroom teacher (or meeting leader).

If a classroom meeting is conducted to address individual students' behaviour it will be important to consider whether their self-esteem might be overly affected by hearing what their fellow students might say — particularly if there is any 'latent hostility'.

Can that latent hostility be tempered by the teacher's leadership in an open forum? Will students choose not to contribute due to anxiety over possible 'retribution'? The solving of such matters can be helped by discussing these concerns with senior colleagues before conducting such a meeting.

If a student (on a behaviour recovery plan) does sit in on this type of meeting it will help to have the student sitting next to the teacher. It will also be important to explain to the student why this special meeting is being held, emphasising that his fellow students want to share their concerns and help.

Because such a meeting is targeted around an individual student and his behaviour it will be advisable to:

- check with senior staff first
- consider whether or not to inform the parent(s), noting that' ... we have classroom meetings regularly in our class (as you know). We also have meetings to discuss concerns about each individual's learning and behaviour. These meetings are to share concerns and offer class-wide support ...'

  If the parent rejects any notion of a classroom meeting to discuss *their* child's behaviour (suspecting a 'kangaroo court'!) it will be advisable not to go ahead with such a meeting. Most parents, however, are supportive of anything the school can do to help.

- It is also advisable to ask the student in question if he would like to be present or not. If he is not comfortable (about joining in) he can spend time in another classroom and the teacher can report back to him at a later stage.

Meeting times generally run from twenty to thirty minutes (longer at middle school). It is normally preferable to conduct a meeting in the last twenty to forty minutes of a classroom period. The teacher opens the meeting by clarifying the special reason for it being held: 'I've called this special meeting because there is a problem in our class and we need to talk about it together, so we can find helpful ways to fix it'. The teacher will continue on to specifically describe the behaviours that are working against the fair rules 'of our class'. If the child is in the room he will connect, as will all the other children who behave this way from time to time. Some students may quickly 'cotton-on' — naming the student who is causing concern. 'That's Darren! He *always* calls out.'

If any member of the class group names a particular student, the teacher should follow up such a response in a non-threatening way: 'What is it that (student's name) does that upsets, annoys, concerns you or makes it unsafe for others?' Encourage comment on behaviour (addressing the behaviour, not attacking the person). At all times the teacher will enforce the no put-down rule. The group will need some time to discuss the kind of behaviours that the student does and why such behaviour concerns them. No judgement should be made, just clarify the behaviours and give the whole class the opportunity to share how it feels about *this* kind of behaviour. Not all students will wish to contribute. If the student — in question

— wants to have his say he should be encouraged — some students are quick to defend their behaviour, others will sulk and remain quiet.

There will be some natural whingeing by classroom members about 'the difficult student'. This is normal and allowable; the teacher will refocus this (within the rules) and not let it degenerate into put-downs.

It will help if the teacher keeps a record of *key* comments, behaviours (and their effects) on a whiteboard as the meeting progresses. This can give a focus to the key question, 'Why do you think *some* students behave like this?'

After five minutes or so, the teacher can ask, 'Why do you think some students (or the named student) behave like this (be specific)? Let's go around the group one at a time.'

Children are quite effective at playing amateur psychologist when it comes to *other people's* behaviour. 'He does that (roll on the floor, jump in the big dust bin, push in line) because he wants us all to laugh at him'; 'He thinks that's smart!'; 'He's just showing off and he wants us to notice him all the time.' Children can often identify the goals of disruptive behaviour well (attention-seeking, power-seeking, revenge and withdrawal). Some can even recognise the active and passive aspects of each of these 'mistaken goals' as categorised by Dreikurs (1968) and Dreikurs et al. (1982).

It's worth discussing as a caveat: 'All of us (from time to time) do annoying or silly things. We don't *always* behave well. We forget and sometimes we, too, break the rules. The difference with some children (consider here whether to name individual students) is that they (or he) do these things (refer to the list on the whiteboard) lots of times and are *often* not following our classroom rules.' Supplementary questions can help here. 'When students roll on the floor, snatch your work, spit or shove, what do we do? If we laugh or hit back what happens?' Allow some discussion on the way our behaviour can affect his (or theirs).

The meeting will need to move towards a focus for peer support. The teacher asks: 'What do you think we can do as a class to help *students who behave like this?*' If the student (on recovery) is in the meeting the teacher can focus the question by naming the student and asking for supportive suggestions. Common responses from children include:

- 'We can remind him ...'
- 'One of us could help him with his work, show him what to do.'
- 'We could remind him about our classroom rules.'
- 'We could tell him what we don't like about what he does.'
- 'We could tell him to stop ...' (It will be important to remind students of helpful ways to 'say their piece' when other students annoy or hassle them.)

- 'Take no notice when he does silly stuff like ...' (Ignore him — this is a very powerful strategy, when it works.)

When students suggest 'ignoring' as a 'strategy' it will be important to discuss the difference between *tactical* ignoring and blind ignorance — between behaviours that can be *appropriately* ignored and those that cannot be ignored. This includes safety infringements, significant teasing, physical aggression or damaging personal (or class) property. Bullying, of any kind, should *never* be ignored.

Students will often raise the need for teacher help, when the student behaves '*really* badly' in class time; they will often advocate the use of time-out if the student does not settle down and work by the fair rules, or if he becomes hostile or aggressive. The class teacher needs to assure the class group that no student has the right to be abusive or aggressive, to bully or keep interrupting others' learning.

If the meeting is flagging, draw the threads together and summarise. 'It looks like the group is saying ...'; 'It looks like we need to ...'; 'We'll close our meeting now ...'; 'We'll meet again next (nominate a time) to discuss this issue some more. Thank you all for sharing and discussing.' Remember, if the class is not used to classroom meetings the first few will be a little strained. Both the class teacher and the students need to get used to open discussion, the ebb and flow of open questions, guided questions, feedback and shared decision-making.

The value of having individual students (on recovery plans) at such a meeting is that they are exposed to peer comment. A further meeting can be arranged where the student (in question) can be offered the opportunity to give a commitment to the class about behaviour change. This is more acutely relevant for older students (see p. 91). This approach has been used successfully on school camps where a student has been hassling others in the dormitory. The class meeting proposes that he leaves the camp if he keeps doing 'x', 'y' or 'z'. The disruptive student then has the opportunity (after he and his peers outline their grievances) to make a commitment to change his behaviour. It will be important — if public commitments are part of classroom meetings — that the other students assist him in forming a change plan. It's one thing to stop certain behaviours, it's another thing to start new behaviours. A student may promise the world, 'I'll never do it again'. What the teacher needs to clarify, here, is 'What can you do *instead*?' and then work with the student on a plan to do it. If a plan cannot be developed at the meeting the normal procedure is for the teacher to take the group's suggestion and initiate a one-to-one session with the student to formulate a behaviour change plan (see Chapter 3).

Classroom meetings should end on a positive note. The teacher sums up the responses to the three major questions:

1   What is the problem?

2   Why do you (we) think we have this problem? or Why do you think student(s) behave like this? (Be specific.)

3   What can we do to fix this problem and how can we help the student(s) to change?

The teacher then clarifies the proposals suggested and lets the group know that there will be another meeting in a week's time if there are any changes following 'our plan'.

Classroom meetings *of all kinds* can be a valuable feature of classroom learning. Children learn to describe, analyse and contribute to solving problems. They are especially valuable in giving students an opportunity to comment on their peers' behaviour(s), how it affects them, and to work on supportive solutions with their teacher.

In one school students were encouraged by their teachers to explore the issue of playground behaviour and concerns that were frequently being raised. A range of suggestions and proposals were offered by students. One of the proposals addressed solving a problem like someone interfering with games or play activities. Each of the following suggestions had a cartoon accompanying it:

- Stop and think; how can I solve this myself?
- Ignore the person (if I'm being teased) and walk away.
- Talk it over with the person. 'Can we please have our ball back?'
- Invite them to join in your game or activity.
- Try to stop the behaviour. 'I don't like it when … please stop.'
- Give them a warning. 'If you keep doing that I'll go and tell the teacher.' 'If the umpire says you're out, you're out. If you can't accept you're out, you can't play the game.'
- Report to a teacher.

In another school the issue of teasing was raised at a classroom meeting. '*What does it mean to tease? Why do people do it? What can we do when we're teased?*' The solutions were similar to the above but one girl raised the old rhyme 'sticks and stones can break my bones but names will never hurt me'. While this rhyme does not carry the whole truth, as the young girl (Year 1) pointed out, she also argued that 'in my head I can be strong — I know I'm not what they say the name is!' And I said 'good on you!' I hope she keeps that cognitive tool well into adulthood.

A classroom meeting: a case study (Grade 1)

One day, when Matt was out of the room (engineered by me in conjunction with the principal as he was rarely absent from school — his mother couldn't stand to keep him at home), I called a class meeting.

I opened the meeting by simply stating what I'd noticed happening in the room. 'I've noticed that some of you are really fed up with the things Matt has been doing.' Then, after seeing nods and sighs, I asked 'What things annoy you the most?' The class and I had a really good clearing of the air. Then I told them some of the desired behaviours I liked him to exhibit; that is, sitting on the mat, putting his hand up and so on. I also asked the class to verbalise some of the things they'd like him to do. Apart from the really annoying things they also raised concerns like 'putting the lids on felt-tipped pens', and 'be nice to us' and 'to say nice things — not hurtful things'.

Once I had them focused on these positives I asked them to recall any times when they had actually caught him being nice. I, of course, gave an example to start them off. It took a bit of prising out but they could relate some instances, when prompted.

Then I asked them what they were doing or saying to Matt when he was being nice. We discussed feelings, particularly anger, and I began to draw parallels between Matt's behaviour and their own, so that they could see how similar he was to them in a lot of ways.

I decided to use the analogy of a key and described the heart as having a door, but in Matt's case it was often locked. I told them that if they open the door to their hearts all the time, wonderful things come out. I focused on a few individuals who have 'model behaviour' and reinforced their good natures. 'I can't see the door to Rebecca's heart but I know it's open because she is smiling.' I then looked at Rebecca and said 'But your door isn't always open like that. When someone says something horrible to you I feel your door close up tight. It's a very unusual door you have in your heart. It works two ways and sometimes the other side opens and the other things come out, and you say something horrible and hurtful. Has anyone ever felt that happen to their door? Why does it happen?'

Note: it is always important to distinguish — as Helen did — between the 'bad' things we say and do (our behaviour), and the essential person. For example, it is not bad to be angry. A person is not 'bad' for having angry feelings, and being angry, though sometimes people behave badly *when* they are angry. Later (in Chapter 7) the distinction is made between 'good' and 'bad' *habits* of anger; the difference between the emotions of anger and what we have typically *learned* to do *when* we are angry.

After discussing cause and effect with them I said, 'Everyone has a key to the door in their heart. The same key fits everybody's door. If you say something nice to a person you unlock their good door and nice things come out. But if you turn the key the other way and say something mean, the other door opens and unhappy (and sometimes bad) things come out. You use your keys on each other really well because I feel the good doors opening all the time. But what about Matt? When his door is open which one is it?' Chorus: 'The bad one'. 'Well, you're the ones with the key to the door of his heart. You can open it. Which way have you been turning the key?' Chorus: 'The wrong way'.

From there it was then a matter of discussing how to turn the key so the good door could open. They came up with heaps of suggestions. For the next six months or more I could solve Matt and peer conflict by saying 'Remember the key?' or by pointing to my chest and pretending to turn a key (a privately understood signal).

The best strategy they came up with was to ignore Matts' attentional behaviour (tactically). They put this into action in an extreme way. I turned around once and saw Matt hitting another child on the head with a book (lightly, intentionally and repeatedly); the child just sat there and 'took it', not reacting at all. Matt didn't get the attention he was after and gave up. I praised the victim for using his 'key'. After a while Matt was getting more attention for his good behaviour than his bad. It was also a good reminder to me to stay positive with him.

He now sits attentively on the mat, raises his hand and is quite a popular member of the class. The 'key analogy' operates without anyone having to think about it. His self-esteem is excellent. I can't change his home environment but he feels safe at school. The key concept is fairly abstract but a key itself is concrete. By having an imaginary key and a concrete cue, children were reminded to stay positive and ignore where possible (and where appropriate) what they'd didn't like.

Needless to say, Matt will live in my memory forever (see also p. 3).

Helen: primary school teacher

A classroom meeting and playground behaviour: a case study

Here is an example of a classroom meeting approach called 'group' from a multi-age classroom (Years 3–6).

In the playground, as in any playground, some children were often mistreating others: fighting, name-calling, teasing and generally not respecting each child's rights. As in every school playground, not all children displayed this behaviour. The children were invited to take part in something called 'group'. During 'group', children are required to sit in a circle at the same level (that is, all on the floor or all on chairs) and to follow certain rules.

1 *During group meetings, children are free to comment on positive and negative things affecting their lives on and off the playground, such as 'I like it when ...' or 'I don't like it when ...'*

2 *When commenting on or raising an issue, children are required to speak directly to the offending party/parties.*

3 *If a particular child has been taken to task over an offending behaviour that child then has the right to reply.*

4 *An appointed child named as Facilitator directs each session. This position is rotated so that each child experiences the role.*

5 *When someone is speaking, everyone else listens and awaits their turn to speak. This comes under the jurisdiction of the Facilitator.*

6 *Once a problem/issue has been openly discussed by both parties and the offending behaviour identified, the Facilitator invites other children to respond. Solutions for and/or consequences of a repeat of that same behaviour are then suggested by group members. These are then discussed and voted on. The solution most favoured by the children is recorded in a group book so that a record is kept of all decisions made. These decisions are binding until the group decides to amend them. Children may refer to this book at any time.*

7 *Participants must be prepared to speak the truth at all times during these sessions.*

8 *The rights of each participant must be protected by the teacher at all times.*

Initially, confident children were the first to raise issues with the group. As time wore on all children realised that each person was being listened to and playground bullies were being held accountable for what they were doing. Gradually, other issues were raised, such as name-calling or using other people's property without asking permission and so on. What really consolidated the authority of the group was that their solutions and recommended courses of action were binding in and out of the classroom. After five weeks of 'group', two or three times a week, the children realised that something more was needed.

The Arbitrating System

Some children were still coming to teachers to solve their problems while others didn't dare for fear of retribution from others. One child raised this point (during group), and an extremely productive discussion began. At the completion of this session the children had effectively given birth to what is *now known as the Arbitrating System. The system involves three stages of conflict resolution in and out of the classroom for all students, and the teacher, to follow.*

Stage 1
Try to solve the conflict yourself. For example, if someone calls you a name you don't like ask them not to call you that name again. The second child then is not allowed to refer to you in that manner again. If they do, you may move on to Stage 2.

Stage 2
Go to either of the Arbitrators (one boy, one girl; it is important to have a different pair each week so that everyone gets a turn) and explain what has happened. That Arbitrator then decides on the consequences of each party's actions and outlines consequences to any guilty party in proportion to their offence(s). Suggested consequences or courses of action are listed in the group book as decided on during group meetings and the Arbitrators may refer to this book when they are unsure of what consequences to give. If the Arbitrator is uncertain as to how to proceed, or if any of the parties feel that they have been treated unfairly they may move to Stage 3.

Stage 3
Any party not satisfied that they were given a fair hearing may approach the teacher. The teacher will then listen to each party and proceed as follows.

- *If the Arbitrator is uncertain, the teacher will then listen and ask how they think they should proceed. The idea is to encourage them to take risks and back their own judgement. Teachers try to guide them into making a decision rather than take over.*
- *If one of the parties feels that the Arbitrator has not done his/her job in a fair manner they may approach the teacher. The teacher's job is to listen and, if an injustice has been done, justice will prevail.*
- *If a child is trying to 'put one over' the teacher, that student gets twice the original consequence.*
- *If the Arbitrator genuinely did his/her best, but was not able to arbitrate fairly, the teacher has the responsibility to speak one-to-one with that child so that he/she knows how to proceed under similar circumstances.*
- *If the Arbitrator deliberately neglected his/her responsibilities, the teacher will work one-to-one to impart an understanding of why the arbitrators must do their job to the best of their abilities each time a child comes to them for assistance.*

Arbitrators learn on the job and need constant back-up and support until they can function on their own. It is important that teachers do not take over but guide the arbitrators to make fair decisions.

Ciaran: teacher in multi-age primary classroom

This model can only be developed and utilised when the class has had significant and ongoing experience with such classroom meetings and mediation/arbitration support. This model relies on a high level of trust, and some natural risk and reflective teacher monitoring and encouragement over time.

Disciplining Children with Emotional Behavioural Disorders

6

Effective discipline of children with behaviour disorders is not significantly different from the sort of positive disciplinary practices typical children respond to. As Kounin and Obradovic (in Robertson 1989) have noted, emotionally disturbed children in normal schools respond to techniques of good classroom management in the same way as 'non-disturbed' children.

Discipline is effectively leading, guiding and teaching children to own (and be responsible for) their behaviour in the context of respecting others' rights (Rogers 1998). The elements of effective and positive discipline involves a challenging balance between prevention, correction, encouragement, support and repairing and rebuilding.

It is important for all students, especially at the establishment phase of the year, to be aware of the classroom rules for behaviour and the routines for the class. These include routines for activities such as how to enter and leave the classroom, move around the class, clean up materials, move on to the mat (during whole-class instructional/discussion time), moderate working noise and packing up.

It is a good idea to publish the rules using class drawings or illustrations. Make the rules few in number, simple, enforceable and as positively stated as possible. Key headings used for classroom rules can focus on:

- To learn well in our class we ...
- To feel safe in our class we ...
- To show respect and thoughtful manners we ...

Many primary teachers use the concept of a *classroom behaviour agreement* (or plan) that outlines the core rights, responsibilities and rules of the classroom community. This 'agreement' also outlines the basic consequences for 'breaking the rules', the emphasis being that when rule-breaking behaviour occurs it affects other students' rights to learn; to feel safe and to enjoy basic respect of person, place and property (Rogers 1998). 'Rule-breaking' that occasions behaviour consequences is not merely calling out, butting in, or natural kinaesthetic behaviour — it is when a student *repeatedly* behaves in ways that affect other students' (and the teacher's) rights.

By referring the student's plan to *our class rules* the teacher establishes continuity and consistency of fair behaviour between the individual and the classroom group.

Consequences for rule-breaking also need to be outlined in the first week of term one; especially the use of time-out provisions. Preventative measures also need to include appropriate (and considered) seating for students (with EBD); modified task requirements need to be achievable, sequenced with appropriate materials and resources, and include a balance of group and individual learning tasks. *Individual* task sheets for these students can provide a positive framework within which success can be monitored and progress demonstrated (see PM 17*c* in the appendix).

Corrective discipline

Corrective discipline considers what is said, and done, to address distracting and disruptive behaviour. Teachers need to consider how to correct:

- without being long-winded
- without over-servicing attention-seeking or power-seeking by the child (especially in front of the child's peers)
- without using sarcasm, embarrassment, intentional public shaming or persistent criticism
- by addressing the problem behaviour (and not attacking the person).

This is a tall order. These basic protocols, though, are essential in maintaining a positive corrective climate for *all* students, not just students with EBD.

When we are angry with students' behaviour or when we have to use unambiguous command language (such as in safety settings) we can be clear about our anger without intentionally belittling the child. There are a number of strategies that can be adopted which help develop this positive climate.

- It is useful to give commands with a brief, sharp, attention-getting tone (lift the voice) then drop to a firm, assertive voice and posture to give the actual command. For example, 'Michael (raise the voice then pause), move over there now' (said in a normal voice). The command can be *repeated* if he still doesn't move. A few words said again are better than many words said in a high-pitched angry voice. That unsettles the audience as well as the target student.

- It is not easy to calm a recalcitrant child when a teacher is speaking loudly, or shouting, or threatening or grabbing and shaking the child ('Wake up to yourself and do what I say!'). While it is appropriate to *raise* the voice at times it is important to then drop the voice (when attention is gained) and speak in a firm, clear, slower, decisive voice. If a teacher *keeps* the voice at the same level of sharpness and loudness she is very likely to exacerbate further hostility (or aggression) in the disruptive child, and create unnecessary anxiety in the children observing the fracas!

    One of the hardest principles of behaviour leadership is to remember that the first person 'to calm' in a conflict (or potential conflict) is not the child but the adult (the teacher). It is even harder to 'remember' this *in the emotional moment*! 'Calm' in this sense is not some passive, quiescent, behaviour in the teacher; it is keeping a sense of focused control *in the situation*. Such 'calmness' is not inconsistent with the need to be appropriately assertive where necessary.

    It is easy to make judgements about teachers who shout, who vilify a child (using sarcasm and public embarrassment) or who speak threateningly — some students behave in ways that are extremely stressful to teacher leadership. It takes *conscious* skill (preventative planning) to be respectively assertive (clear and unambiguously firm) and respectful. The ability to be assertive is not based in mere personality; it is a skill and can be learned.

- Positive correction considers what is said, and how it is said, in discipline transactions both in content and 'tone'. Sarcasm, hostility, threats and aggression can all be conveyed in language tone with proximity and bodily gesture (such as pointing at a student — or even his work — with the 'hostile finger'). Coming side-on to a student during on-task correction is less threatening (in tone and gesture) than coming face-on and pointing.

A discipline plan

Most teachers plan well for their day-to-day teaching activities and lessons. Some teachers forget that the same kind, and level, of planning is also appropriate for our daily discipline. A teacher's *discipline plan is* a conscious framework of intervention (particularly our discipline and language) when he or she needs to remind, correct or even confront a child who is behaving in distracting or disruptive ways. A discipline plan is a conscious, reflective framework of 'intervention' that increases the likelihood that the aims of discipline will be addressed (even met!).

Discipline aims

- Enables the child, once corrected, to 'own' his behaviour and to respect others' rights to learn and feel safe.
- Enables students to come back on task as quickly as possible. The purpose of discipline is not merely to stop distracting or disruptive behaviour alone, it is to re-engage the student to the 'core business' of classroom teaching and learning.
- Any discipline needs to be based in the core rights and responsibilities expressed in the classroom behaviour agreement (p. 95).
- All students have a *right to learn* without distraction or disruption.
- All students have a *right to respect* and *fair treatment* (this includes one's property as well as one's person).
- All students have a *right to feel safe here* (this includes psychological as well as physical safety). Put-downs 'cheap shots', hurtful teasing and swearing at others are unacceptable. Bullying of any kind is totally unacceptable.

In the establishment phase of the year the teacher will have covered these rights (and their *responsibilities)* carefully through group discussion and rule-clarification. Having aims and having a published (age-related) behaviour agreement with the class that addresses rights, rules, responsibilities and consequences is never enough. It is the *basis* for positive behaviour and fair discipline.

A discipline plan also includes a teacher having a conscious plan for addressing the typical range of distracting and disruptive behaviour, so that his or her corrective discipline is as positive as possible, avoids reactive responses and is likely to meet the aims noted above.

Discipline behaviour

A discipline plan enables a teacher to intervene *least intrusively* (where possible), moving to *more intrusive* as is necessary. Being 'more intrusive' does not mean being more hostile (and should never imply aggressive tone, manner or language). 'A more intrusive' stance implies being assertive in a matter appropriate to the context.

The language of correction

As noted earlier, language is significant in one's *characteristic* discipline. It is my view that we ought to reflect on our characteristic language of correction (Rogers 1998) in reference to our discipline and management. Of course words are never *mere* words; the *meaning, intent, confidence* and *expectation* within our language is carried by our characteristic tone, manner and body language. Some examples include:

- When correcting, teachers avoid overuse 'no', 'can't', 'mustn't' and don't'. 'Don't use the scissors stupidly' can become, 'Use the scissors carefully.' In effect, it is learning to say 'do' more than 'don't'. It is always easier to tell a student what he shouldn't be doing, rather than what he should be doing.

  If Ibrahim and Troy are being silly with the window blinds, a teacher's direction/reminder needs to focus on *expected* behaviour: 'Ibrahim and Troy ...' Allow some very brief tactical pausing (...) to engage eye-contact. 'You're fiddling with the window blinds (give a *brief* description). Leave the blinds and face this way. Thanks.' (This is a *behavioural* direction — in contrast to 'Don't fiddle with the blinds!')

  When giving corrective directions it will help to:
  - focus on the *desired* behaviour (where possible)
  - use action language (verbs or participles) — 'Troy, hands and feet *in your lap* and *facing* this way' (This is said to a child who is overly fidgety.) In this example a simple non-verbal cue is also very effective. For example, 'Michael *hands up* (without calling out) Thank you.' Negative caveats are always balanced by positive rule expectation
  - keep the corrective language brief (where possible)
  - give appropriate take-up-time to the student (rather than staring him into submission). This is very important for older students.

The teacher sees Craig time-wasting at his table during on-task learning time (he's surreptitiously playing with a small toy). Rather than simply take, or snatch, the toy the teacher gives a *directed choice*. 'I notice you're playing with that little skateboard, Craig. I want you to put it in your locker tray or on my table. I'll come and check your work later.' Her tone is positive and expectant (very few students put the *objet d'art* on the teacher's table!). If the student refuses to put the toy away the teacher will use an immediate, or a *deferred* consequence (p. 103).

- Task reminders: when giving task reminders or instructions to the individual student it is important not to overload the child's short-term memory. A list can help (pp. 74–5).

  Encourage eye-contact by standing close to the child (at his level). *Any* task reminders will benefit (the group or individual) from eye-contact followed by brief, clear and succinct (and as simple as possible) direction or task-reminder. It can also help the individual child to remember the task by asking him to repeat it back to check/monitor for comprehension (the visual reminder card on his desk will also help; for example, this list on pp. 74–5).

  Many children will respond positively to private non-verbal cues that can act as quiet and quick reminders for coming back on-task (p. 48). One I've used for many years with older students is 'nose to the grindstone' (sounds painful), catching their eye (without using their name). I make a brief, small, L-shaped signal near my nose and then a small circle in the air with my index finger — followed by a wink.

  If the child (at lower/middle primary) has a peer helper he, too, can quietly remind the child of his task and task progress (p. 76).

- If a student wants to change activities before the appropriate completion it can help to use conditional language: 'Yes — *when*' is more likely to invite co-operation than 'No you can't work on ... *because* you haven't finished ...'

- Direct questions such as: 'What?' 'When?' 'How?' or 'Where?' are more effective than 'Why?' questions.

Asking a child why he is calling out is unnecessary and ineffective (young children may not 'know'). With older children, interrogatives like '... *are you* talking?', or 'You shouldn't be talking, *should you*?' or '*Why* are you talking?' only breed wasted counter-refutation or blame-shifting ('I wasn't the only one talking.')

A direct question helps the child to focus on *what* he should be doing, or *what* the fair rule is ... or *where* he should be now. It expects and invites ownership. If the child does not answer the question, the teacher can give the answer as a direction, 'You need to be ...' or a reminder 'Our rule for ... is ...'

Two students are being silly with their rulers (sword-fighting). The teacher calls over one of them and asks, 'George, what are you doing?' (Her voice is firm — not nasty — her eye-contact stable.) The child says, 'Nothing!' (in a sulky voice). The teacher gives brief and descriptive feedback: 'I saw you hitting Timmy with your ruler'. 'But we were only muckin' 'round', whines George. (The teacher *tactically* ignores his sulking whine and marginal eye-contact.) She replies with a secondary question. 'What are you supposed to be doing?' (This directs and focuses the student's attention on the present on-task issue rather than on secondary issues.) He is required to suggest the appropriate behaviour (or solution), with the teacher's help, if necessary. 'Our work', sighs George (again, she *tactically* ignores this sighing behaviour and keeps the focus on the primary issue at this point ...). 'Off you go then, I'll come and check in a moment.' She gives George a brief directional touch on the arm as he goes back to his seat. A little later she notices him actually working at his table. She gently calls across to George, who looks annoyed. 'What?' The teacher at this point gives him an 'OK' sign with her hand to encourage his on-task behaviour and George sighs and smiles back.

For this teacher the way she engages students in discipline situations is purposeful, not accidental. She also knows it is essential to *re-establish positive working relationships* ASAP. Any corrective discipline should be followed up by some re-establishing after the student has settled back to his task, or followed the teacher's directions or reminder. This re-establishing can be as basic as the example noted (a smile, the 'OK' sign, or that brief word of encouragement). It will also mean starting each day *afresh* with students, particularly students with emotional behaviour disorders.

There are times when a teacher needs to use unambiguous, assertive and commanding language (that is, in safety situations; see also p. 97).

Command language needs to be brief and firm, often with a raising of the voice (to gain immediate attention — *without* shouting). Sometimes a simple and firm stop message is appropriate. 'Stop' messages need to be brief and quickly followed by a direction or direct question in a firm, positive tone. 'Stop that. What is the problem David, Paul?' Minimise loud replies from students by reminding them to speak in 'reasonable' voices. If the students argue they will need to be calmly and firmly re-directed to the fair rule or expected behaviour.

Rule reminders are the most common 'corrective currency' of teachers. It can help to phrase rule reminders with inclusive language ('our', 'us', 'we', 'all ...', 'everyone here ...'). These include:

- 'We've got a rule for ...'
- 'Remember our rule for ...'
- 'What's our rule for ...?' (The direct question, here, invites the student to own the fair, appropriate, rule behaviour.)

For example, a couple of students are arguing over who took whose rubber. The teacher reminds the students: 'Simon and Ahmed (...), we have a rule for settling problems, use it, thanks.' It is important — at this point — that the teacher avoids getting drawn into disputes over property or friendship. If children refuse to take turns, the teacher will remind them of the *sharing rule* or *manners rule*, but avoid asking who started it or why they are arguing over the felt-tipped pens. 'We have a rule for ... (remind them briefly without a lecture). Use it, thanks.' The class will know (from the class rule) that arguing or fighting in class is not acceptable. The class rule will state: 'If you argue or fight you'll be reminded of the rule. If you do not stop you'll have to work separately or have cool-off time'. Children need to learn they can't effectively deal with problems when they are really frustrated, angry or even overly anxious. These problems are more effectively dealt with *after* cool-off time (p. 107).

One of the more difficult principles of behaviour leadership is to keep the corrective intervention focused on the *primary* issue, behaviour or rule. It is so easy to get drawn into a student's 'secondary behaviours' such as arguing about 'Who did what first?'; 'Others were doing that too!'; 'I'm not the only one!'; 'Anyway other teachers don't care if we chew gum, or sit with our mates, or dance on the tables ...'

Teachers often find a student's non-verbal 'secondary behaviour' very irritating, as with the over-done sigh, or when a student raises his eyes to the ceiling and mutters something (in a sibilant whinge), and when he screws his face into a pout ... It can often be helpful — in the immediate emotional moment — to *tactically* ignore such behaviour, keeping the primary focus on the expected behaviour (now) or the fair rule.

When students want to 'argue the point', it is often better (in the emotional moment) to redirect rather than make it a contest. For example:

- 'Other teachers don't care if we ...'
  'I can check that with them.' (This partially acknowledges — without calling the student a liar and refocuses) '... our class rule is ...'
- 'He started it.'
  'I can see you are upset by ... I can check that later' (partial acknowledgement 'dignifying' that possibility) — 'What do you need to be doing now? How can I help?'

If a student continues to argue ̶ ̶ ̶ ̶ ̶ ̶llenge, the consequences, immediate or deferred, need to be ma̶ ̶ ̶ ̶ ̶ ̶ ̶ ̶

Sometimes students need to be respectfully directed with a 'choice' that is immediate or deferred. Immediate consequences refer to safety situations or occasions when students are repeatedly distracting others. These refer generally to some form of 'time-out' (either in the classroom or completely away from the host classroom, see below).

Where possible a 'choice' is given before a consequence like time-out. 'If you continue to annoy others by poking and pushing ... you'll have to sit away over there ...' This is said to an infant child who is poking and touching a fellow student while the teacher is talking to the class group.

When a teacher makes a consequence clear to a student he will sometimes reply, 'I don't care!' While it's tempting to say 'You will care you little s____! I'll make you care!' Hostile reactions only reinforce attentional or power-seeking behaviour. A brief, clear and calm, 'I care — I expect you to care.' Is enough. Sometimes children will say they hate us. They — mostly — don't mean it. It is enough to tell them we do not like what they said. 'If you are really angry tell me in *another* way. I want to help.'

Faber and Mazlish (1980) make the point that it is important not to simply deny children's feelings (particularly their stressful, 'bad' feelings) or to say that such children are bad for poorly expressing such feelings. '... it is important that we give our children a vocabulary for their inner reality. Once they have the words for what they're experiencing they can begin to help themselves' (p. 18).

Sometimes a consequence needs to be *deferred* to a later stage after class time, and when things have calmed down.

Behaviour consequences

All students need to know the general consequences for repeatedly distracting or disruptive behaviour. These consequences will have been discussed with the class, by the teacher and during the establishment phase of the year when they are developing the classroom rules (p. 96). The consequences include:

- work *away* from others (relocation in the room)
- cool-off time (in the room)
- losing recess time (the consequence at recess time can then be negotiated p. 104)
- exit from the room (if the behaviour is repeatedly disruptive, dangerous or unsafe).

Negotiated consequences need to clarify specific future behaviour. This is the essence of behaviour recovery in that it specifies the off-task and on-task behaviour and avoids accepting responses like 'I'll be good now' or 'I won't do it again'. Behaviour recovery emphasises the positive behavioural alternatives. It is important to make clear to the students (and the parents) that consequences are not mere punishments. Students choose their behaviour; positive discipline approaches help students to make better choices. It is in this context any consequences are applied.

A consequence needs to be *as related as possible* and delivered by the teacher in a non-threatening way (the teacher's manner, tone of voice and body language is important). If the teacher applies a consequence with a lecture about the student's behaviour it will be *that* aspect of the consequence the child will likely remember; for example, 'How many times have I told you, eh?! I'm sick and tired of your stupid clowning behaviour in class. It's not funny and you can wipe that stupid smile off your face now! You could be enjoying playtime couldn't you? No — not you — you've got to be *different*, haven't you?'

It is the *certainty* of the consequence that is more effective than its severity. A consequence needs to teach the student something about the appropriate behaviour (that is, gain some *related connection* between behaviour and outcome). If a child damages equipment (or hurts someone) an apology of itself is insufficient. The student can be directed to a time/trade consequence — give his own time to do several positive tasks (civic duty). The responsibility of the consequence should lie with the child, not just the supervising teacher. The student needs to be asked what he needs to do 'to fix things up'. It is more likely the student will 'own' his consequence this way.

Some of the questions we can ask, later and one-to-one are:

- 'What happened?'
- 'What rule (or right) was broken?'
- 'What can you do to fix things up or make them better?'
- 'Which of these solutions is best?'
- 'How can you do it? How can I help?'

Those who 'resist' the consequences

It is worth remembering the obvious, that a student can't be *made* to do anything (thankfully most students are co-operative). Some consequences are, of course, best carried out after appropriate cool-off time; forcing consequences when the child is overly anxious, frustrated or angry may force the child into an unnecessary power struggle. Apart from essential use of exit and time-out provisions (which will need to be immediate) some consequences can often be deferred until the heat has gone down to avoid unnecessary resistance from our students (p. 106).

Keeping running records

As with literacy and numeracy, behaviour development needs regular reflection by the teacher through descriptive assessment. In short, checking if the 'recovery' programme is supporting the process of behavioural change. This also provides basic documentation to administration, parent and support personnel (psychologists, social workers and so on), should formal inquiry processes be necessary.

A simple pro forma can be utilised covering:

- what behaviours are disruptive (be specific)
- what behaviours are specifically targeted for change
- frequency and intensity (see PM 1 in the appendix)
- what programme has been developed to address the disruptive behaviour (be specific)
- how the student typically responds to teacher direction, teacher discipline and teacher encouragement (within his plan).

A simple journal or pro forma can be drawn up that is filled in two or three times a day (after each class session, if possible). A checklist against which a few words of explanation are made is a most efficient method. Even the picture card plan is itself a piece of descriptive feedback for the child, the teacher and the parent (p. 49–50).

Teachers can use these questions to evaluate a student's progress within his behaviour recovery plan:

- In what ways has the student's behaviour changed since introducing behaviour recovery? (Be specific.)
- Is there a noticeable reduction in frequency and intensity of distracting and disruptive behaviour?
- What have other teachers (specialist teachers) noticed?
- Can the teacher, if she has a workable relationship with the child's caregivers, ask them if they too have noticed any changes in their child's attitude and behaviour towards school?
- How has the student responded to the daily/weekly feedback and evaluation?

- Have any reward schedules been more effective than others?
- What are the most workable features of the programme with respect to this student?
- Has there been regular discussion with team colleagues while using the programme?
- What areas (specifically) can be improved?

Structural support: time-out

These are occasions when a student's behaviour is so disruptive (or dangerous) that the only appropriate intervention is to direct the child to time-out. Repeated and intrusive disruptive behaviour is stressful to teacher and class alike. No teacher should have to be in the invidious position of having a child behave in ways that effectively 'hold a class to ransom'. In the *short-term*, time-out is an essential feature of whole-school discipline policy.

Teachers and students should not have to tolerate back-to-back disruption or hostile or aggressive behaviours directed to person or property. It is an essential feature of a classroom discipline plan (and of behaviour recovery in particular) that class teachers are *supported* by having a well planned time-out policy and process.

Time-out policy

These key questions should be answered collaboratively by staff within a whole-school staff policy on time-out:

- What sorts of behaviours would we normally expect to use time-out for?
- How can we utilise time-out *within the classroom*? Many infant and middle primary teachers have in-class time-out options to give the offending student 'cool-off time' and 'thinking' time.
- When we exit for time-out what is the best way we can do it? Even particular forms and expressions of language can be helpful here. Many schools have a school-wide 'form' of language that teachers use when directing a student from the classroom 'to' time-out.
- What if the child refuses to go? What is our support plan? (See below.)
- Where does the child go?
- What happens to the child when he gets to the time-out place? (Do we use a colleague's room for time-out, a special time-out room or area, or the deputy principal's office?)

- What is reasonably required of the child before coming back to his home classroom?

The essential feature of time-out (at any level) is that it gives the child (and the teacher?) time to cool down after a significantly disruptive incident and regain some self-control. All the children in the class need to know that cool-off time will be carried out when children make it difficult for others to feel safe, to learn and to be treated with respect. Time-out (and in class cool-off time) is withdrawal time from the group until the child has settled and agrees to work by the fair rules. The professional discretion of what behaviour constitutes a significant breach of rights needs to be discussed and decided on by all staff so that time-out becomes part of a known school-wide process.

Staff, students and parents need to recognise that time-out is a consequence (not primarily a punishment). It should be designed and utilised so that the child sees a *connection* between his disruptive behaviour and the outcome (time-out). It is especially important for parents to understand what is meant by time-out so that they are not conjuring up images of standing in corners or sitting in some tiny cubicle!

Time-out is normally a short-term process that needs the secondary back-up of other consequences and remediation processes. Time-out, by itself, rarely changes disordered behaviour. The key to the use of time-out is the employment of the certainty principle. Teachers don't need to yell at or drag the child heatedly out of the room. In fact, the more dignity and calm that can be retained, the more effective the consequence. The message to the student is, 'Whenever you act this way (be specific) this is what will happen'.

Time-out is also not a reward; the child should not be given special privileges or be asked why he did 'x', 'y' or 'z'. Nor should he receive counselling or special jobs or tasks *at that time*. I have seen children given special jobs immediately following exit, and time-out, from the classroom. It is also unhelpful to engage the student in a counselling process following the disruptive behaviour for which they were directed to time-out. They often associate, then, the pleasant experiences with their disruptive behaviours. Time-out ought to be as non-reinforcing as possible.

I have had children kick and scream during time-out, but have not restrained them unless it is essential. At this point it is important to give the out-of-control student the calm reassurances that we'll release them when they 'calm' and 'settle' (p. 112). The child's return to the room should be carried out quietly, calmly and within agreed time schedules. For example, if a child goes to time-out twenty minutes before recess it may be appropriate to have him out of the classroom *until* recess.

Cool off time in the classroom (at infant–middle primary level)

It may be appropriate to have a *cool-off* time in the room if the child is unduly unsettled and reserve exit/time-out (from the room) for the more significant rights-infringing behaviours. The main point is that children know the limits and expectations of behaviour, and connect their experience in time-out *to* their disruptive behaviour. This process is explained to all the children in the establishment phase of the year. That is, if they are making it difficult for others to learn or feel safe they will either be

Take 5

directed to work away from others for a period of time (relocation in the room), have some special (and non-reinforcing) cool-off time to settle and think about their responsibility, or be directed to leave the room until they are ready to work by the classroom rules.

It may be possible to give a child a directed choice (on some occasions) before directing them to time-out; that is, 'If you continue to ... (be specific) then you'll have to go to time-out.'

It is pointless arguing or debating with students about their behaviour in front of an audience (it only feeds their attention-seeking or power-engaging behaviours). Some teachers use a special place in the room for cool-off time. The child is initially taken there with only a *brief* conditional reminder, 'When you've stopped feeling angry inside then you can come back to work at your table'. We need to make clear to the student that there is nothing wrong with the angry feeling, but when a child throws things around the table, or pushes, or pokes, or slaps others, then there is a related and certain consequence of cool-off-time.

Some infant teachers place an egg-timer in the cool-off time area. The student can choose to come back on his own accord when he's settled and prepared to work within fair rules (a five-minute egg-timer can be placed on a small table with a few cushions for the child to sit on).

It is crucial, though, that the teacher conducts the process of time-out (as a consequence) calmly; without yelling.

Supported exit and time out from the classroom

When I first began teaching I did some relief work in a number of difficult schools. I recall, on one occasion, a very testy Year 6 class. Within ten minutes one of the boys threw what was later described as a characteristic 'major wobbly'. He ran around the room several times and then hopped out of the window. (First floor!) I felt helpless partly because I didn't know what to do — I was unprepared — and also because I had no idea from senior staff that such (apparently typical behaviour) might happen with this student.

Over the years I've come across countless situations like this where teacher stress, behaviour monitoring and protection of all students' rights could have been effectively handled within a whole-school approach to the use of time-out.

It is *generally* not advisable to have the student sitting outside the classroom as a form of time-out, especially students with emotional behavioural disorder. This merely gives them an audience one door's length away! If the area just outside the door is used, it should be for a short spell (five minutes) with a clear 'When ... then ...' message as the parting words. For example, 'When you've settled down then you're welcome to come back to your seat.' It is not also advisable for staff who pass by such students in the corridor to question them (or talk with them), but rather to leave them in 'time-out mode'.

Many challenging students will not stand outside the room anyway, and some will not even leave the room and go to the designated person or place when directed by the teacher. The direction to leave the room, will be resisted or simply provoke further acting out behaviour. Many schools use a basic school-wide 'cue-system': a small red card (with the room number on) pinned to the wall or chalkboard. In a situation that requires a student exit from the room, the card can be sent, with a reliable student, to either a nominated teacher, a senior teacher, or the deputy principal (all planned ahead of time within the school's supportive time-out policy). One of the nominated teachers can then, on receipt of the card, go to that room and direct the child to 'Leave the room, come with the

teacher …' Another option that works well is to direct the student by name, adding, 'I'll see you in my office in a few minutes'. The exit process needs to be carried out calmly with an expectant tone.

On *rare* occasions even the presence of another teacher to direct the said student away from the classroom (for time-out) will meet a blatant refusal — the student sits down, or lies down and screams. On these occasions it is worth taking the whole class out calmly, leaving behind their work. They can go for a walk around the building or play an ad hoc game or activity. This immediately *removes the audience* from the disruptive student long enough for him to connect that the audience has gone. This crisis intervention option must be a pre-planned, school-wide policy option. A senior teacher stays with the highly disruptive student while the regular class teacher 'exits the class'. The support colleague can then direct the disturbing student away to an alternative time-out place.

In small schools the support colleague is often teaching at the time their assistance is required. In this case the teacher who comes to exit will have to be spatially close so she can leave her class (with door open) to briefly walk across and escort the highly disruptive student back to her own classroom (away from the original audience).

The school should have in place a crisis time-out option, even if it is used rarely. Parent contact should follow such uses of time-out.

Time-out, itself, may modify behaviour, providing, of course, that time-out is not reinforced by talking sessions, lectures or special 'privileges'. Counselling and supportive behaviour recovery procedures are arranged for *another* time, and actual time-out should be connected in the student's mind with withdrawal from his peer group as a consequence of his disruptive behaviour and minimal over-servicing by the adult.

There are occasions (rare fortunately) when a teacher will need to physically restrain a child when his behaviour is at serious risk to another student, or to themselves. The issue of appropriateness of physical touch — and the possible restraint occasion — is one that should be discussed within a *whole-school* policy; it should never be left to mere individual discretion. On such occasions the emotional tension is high and rationality is low. Students are often frustrated, angry and display little self-control.

Restraining children who are a significant danger to themselves or others is normally addressed under the frustratingly broad legal maxim of 'appropriate duty-of-care' (we are in *loco parentis!*).[1] In any situation of *potential* crisis it is always advisable to send for a senior colleague, or (at least) a colleague nearby, as both witness and for immediate moral and professional support.

The *paramount right is that of safety*, say, in a serious fight or serious 'horseplay', or in case of serious damage to property, or if a child is about to commit a criminal offence. If students refuse to separate after an unambiguous command the teacher may have to restrain one of the students:

- *Warn before any restraint*, particularly with older students.
- Restraint may be as limited as putting out an arm between students, or across a student's personal space or a directional hand on the back (not pushing). Least intrusive is the key. It may — on occasion — require a holding of the student. Again, staff should have discussed the *difficult practicalities* of 'hold and restrain'.
- Always release the student when he is calmer. During any restraint procedure it is crucial to use a *calm, clear voice* to assure the student that when he 'calms and settles down', we will let go, find out what happened and help them work things out.

- Later, when the student(s) have calmed the teacher can organise for writing up reports, right of reply and (if appropriate) mediation.

It is essential that the teacher formally records clear details of the incident and if there are witnesses (including student witnesses), how the incident progressed, the action of the intervening teacher, the student's response and its outcome, and obviously any details of damage or injury.

Always direct the peer audience away from the danger or melee (they are often waiting for 'permission' to leave the scene) and send for extra adult assistance if there is no other adult in the vicinity (this is crucial in open, playground, settings).

Classroom rotation

There needs to be a distinction made between having a student in a colleague's room to do set work there and the student going to a colleague's room for time-out when he is acting in a significantly disruptive way. Classroom rotation of a student can give the initiating class teacher a breather; this too is a planned process but it is different, in purpose, from time-out. If other teachers complain about supporting a school-wide option for classroom rotation ('Why should I have *him* in my room for a whole period!') it is important to stress how they would appreciate that kind of support in the same situation as their colleague who has this very challenging student day in day out. (They could be in that situation next year!) It goes without saying that forcing a policy of classroom rotation process on staff is counter-productive; staff need to be encouraged not coerced.

The most important caveat

In one sense it is easy for me to write about positive discipline because I don't teach full-time any longer. However, I do remember what it's like being 'boxed-in' with challenging students day in, day out. I've also been in unsupportive schools where the imputation of blame (covert) is on the teacher — that somehow the child's behaviour is the teacher's or parents' fault. I sometimes wonder how I would go at home with a child like that. In my more cynical moments I wonder how some senior staff would cope with challenging students, or a 'reputation' class (the one no one wants!). How would they cope with little or no support? Thankfully schools are much more consciously supportive of colleagues and their needs these days (Rogers 2002).

There are some teachers ill-suited, by personality temperament and lack of reflective experience, to work with very challenging children and children with emotional behavioural disorders.

Most teachers, when faced with challenging student behaviours, work hard — with their colleagues — to find ways to connect. They work with the vagaries of difficult causative factors (pp. 8–11), the pressures of time, and the balancing of rights and responsibilities of *all* their students — not just those with 'special needs'.

Teachers are fallible. If they get any of the approaches and skills mentioned in this book right, on an eight-out-of-ten average they're doing well — very well. Tiredness, frustration ('Will he *ever* learn!') and the often relentless pressure does wear anyone down. The important thing is an awareness matched with effort and backed-up with colleague support. If teachers plan to balance positive correction, within thoughtful preventative follow-up and remediation they will have done their best. And, if they shout, yell or 'lose the plot', from time to time, they will need to forgive themselves and simply (without sycophancy) apologise and rebuild the working relationship between the individual student, or class.

In a supportive school environment, teacher fallibility (like that in our students) is accepted. We do not simply acquiesce to fallibility, but we accept it as part of our human condition.

---

[1] Liability for negligence rests on three elements being satisfied. First, there needs to be a duty to take care. Second, the standard of care required must be breached. Finally, the damage arising must be caused by the breach of duty and must not be too remote from that breach.

The courts have long recognised that teachers owe a duty-of-care to students in their charge. This duty is not limited to refraining from doing things that may lead to a student being injured, but it also obliges a teacher to take positive steps towards maintaining safety.

The *standard* of care that is required cannot be fixed with scientific precision. The law of negligence sets the standard of care as that expected of the reasonable person in the same position. In the school context this means the reasonable teacher armed with the education, skills and insights appropriate for that vocation.

Negligence requires that there be sufficient connection between the breach of duty and the damage. This connection can include a question of causation, if it were highly likely that an injury would have occurred even if all reasonable steps had been taken.

A duty-of-care may then be owed, not only to refrain from injury-creating activities, but to take steps to protect that person from injury. Such a responsibility applies in respect of teachers' duty to students being to subject persons under their control to such reasonable supervision as to prevent injury to other persons. These persons could be other students or outsiders who may reasonably be foreseen as being endangered by a lack of control (Boer and Gleeson 1982, pp. 122–6).

Managing Anger and Bullying Issues

7

Anger is a powerful emotion. In times of high frustration it can easily overtake rational control, even in adults. The exhibition of anger in children expressed in hostile ways towards furniture, property and person is difficult to manage, and can be quite disturbing to teachers, creating anxiety, confusion, even counter-anger.

It is important to consider any emotional pathology contributing to any frequent and ongoing expressions of anger and aggression at school. This needs to be explored with the family and with due assistance from professional support services. The welfare of the class teacher and the other students also needs consideration. If the student's anger pathology is resistant to supportive programmes at the school level of teaching appropriate behaviours, it will be necessary to look at alternative non-school options for the student.

Emotion and expression

It is important to distinguish between the emotion of anger and its expression, and between anger and aggression. Anger itself is not bad per se; it often results from natural, even justifiable, frustration about situations that are difficult, stressful, unfair or unjust. Managing the emotion of frustration in a constructive way is not easy; indeed, many writers have noted that a good deal of the world's problems are caused by the destructive outcomes of anger. Adults, therefore, should appreciate how difficult it is for children to *develop* appropriate coping skills for anger and conflict resolution.

Males seem to be taught (by default as much as 'design') that aggressive expression of anger is legitimate in resolving frustration. Certainly, in some dysfunctional families, hostile or aggressive outcomes of anger are common place. Research on bullying has also shown that there is a correlation between family 'style' and aggressive behaviour (Olweus in Rubin & Pepler 1989; Smith & Thompson 1991).

Children with behaviour disorders, especially, find it difficult to manage frustration and tend to have low frustration tolerance. They tend to be excited in less than helpful ways by their class peers, thus reinforcing their attention-seeking behaviour. If they have a predisposition towards aggressive behaviour they also tend to be 'quick-responding' in social situations. Dodge (1981) observed that aggressive boys misattribute — have a biased attribution — in social settings. They *selectively attend* to the social cues of their peers, putting the worst construction on those cues. Having an *expectancy* that a peer will be hostile, this biased attribution is self-reinforcing, often resulting in retaliatory aggression.

Behaviour recovery will need to address the child's:

- expectancy (which may include maladaptive thinking)
- selective attention to 'hostile' cues or perceived hostile cues ('He stared at me! — that meant he wants to fight!')
- biased weighing on those cues reinforced by (again) maladaptive thinking ('He hates me'; 'He's a _____ because he looks at me.')
- behavioural alternatives to reactive behaviour.

Learned aggression

Researchers have also shown that the frequency and kind of emotional reaction arising with anger is affected by cognition (Eron 1987; Meichenbaum 1977; Bernard & Joyce 1984). Aggressive behaviour is not merely the manifestation of some innate male 'hard-wiring' (or inborn testosterone that is predominantly male!). Aggression is also a learned behaviour. Some children learn (often early in home environments) that aggressive anger gets 'quick results' and can 'shift attention' from personal accountability. At what cost? This question needs to be explained with children as part of the recovery process. Apart from the unacceptable aspects of aggressive anger, the child needs to be aware of 'costs' (to the self and others, including the parent(s)). Male children often learn to think, believe and act aggressively in our society. They learn early that conflict is more readily (and even acceptably) settled by aggressive means. (Macoby & Jacklin 1974, 1980; Rogers 1985).

Smith and Thompson (1991) and Slee (1992) have shown that with attitude change, whole-school policies, clear consequences for bullies, reparative approaches for bullies, support and assertion skills for victims, education of students about non-violent conflict resolution, training of peer mediators, and positive discipline practices, the level of bullying and aggressive behaviour in a school can be significantly reduced. Olweus (1978), in his writing on bullying, has said that the next generation needs to be educated to manage anger constructively. This is the responsibility of school and parents in partnership.

School attitudes about aggression and bullying behaviour need to be realistic but also responsible. 'Boys will be boys ...', 'It's always been with us' and 'It's character building', are just some of the damaging attitudes that perpetuate and 'tolerate' aggression (Rogers 1985). There should be a *whole-school policy focus* clarifying the difference between normal quarrels and 'rough' play, and aggressive behaviour — particularly bullying. Schools have to protect the right to feel and be safe in a school setting — both physical and psychological safety. Turning a 'blind eye' to put-downs; shafting; overt and repeated teasing; purposeful friendship exclusion; name-calling and so on will precipitate a climate where some students believe they can get away with the more physically aggressive features of bullying behaviour. Repeated, selective, intentional hurting (physically or psychologically) over someone weaker should never be tolerated.

There needs to be clear, unambiguous consequences for such behaviour; clear protection and a due support process for the victim (with opportunities to facilitate meetings between bully and victim. Indeed, the degree of support for the victims of aggression — and bullying — in a school is often correlated to the degree of bullying occurring in a school (Slee 1992; Rigby & Slee 1993).

Teaching about anger

Children need to be taught that anger is a feeling. It is not bad to *feel* angry, it's what we normally do when we're angry that counts. It is important that teachers do not make students feel bad about *having* angry feelings. We *all* get angry. We all have a right to our feelings. The harder task is learning to give appropriate and a fair voice to those feelings in ways that are not unfairly aggressive. Especially important is the resolution of conflict in non-aggressive ways that still allow for an expression of appropriate frustration. For example, people should get angry at injustice; what is done with that emotion, however, will determine how effectively some resolution about the injustice is achieved. It is worth noting here, that teachers can have a powerful role in feeding or reducing aggression. I have seen teachers snatch objects from children, yell at them in front of their peers, 'put them down', call them names, invade their personal space and wonder why the child reacts aggressively (verbally or physically). If teachers are angry with children's behaviour it is better to model the behaviour they are seeking to teach their children using these strategies:

- address the behaviour (without attacking the person)
- explain feelings in a clear way without denying frustration or anger (using 'I' statements or 'When/then') 'I am angry because ...'
- with a language of emotion that distinguishes between being 'annoyed', 'irritated' or 'frustrated' (about something) and being angry. *Overuse* of the word angry can devalue its 'currency' and miscue its 'moral weight'. For example, telling a student we're 'angry because he hasn't (repeatedly) done his homework' is inappropriate. We might be annoyed or, more likely, concerned. *Anger* is a power emotion and the *language of anger* needs to be justified in its context and use.

- allow cool-off time when too upset to deal effectively with conflict in the heat of the moment
- learn how to repair and rebuild when students are calmer.

Children (and adults!) can learn that assertion is a way of making their point clearly and as unambiguously as possible. 'I feel upset (or annoyed, or angry) because you push in line instead of waiting' or 'When you push in line I feel annoyed (concerned, upset) because ...' Aggressive anger should be saved for self-defence.

Children can also learn to recognise what it is they get angry over; what is *worth* getting angry about; what they say to themselves when they get angry and after they get angry. They need to be taught (especially through modelling) a vocabulary of anger. There is a difference between annoyed, frustrated, restless, panicky, irritated, displeased, uptight and being angry.

In the following example an infant teacher shares how she developed a behaviour recovery teaching plan for a young girl (4½ years of age) whose hostile and anti-social behaviour was significantly affecting her learning and peer-acceptance. She would often evidence stubborn and angry patterns of behaviour to students and teachers alike. Lisa's behaviour often resulted in her being rejected by her peers and this consequently left her feeling sad.

Anti-social behaviour: a case study

Lisa frequently displayed a range of disruptive behaviours in our classroom group. She had a very short attention span and her listening skills were very poor.

Lisa evidenced little respect for her teachers, her peers and more importantly herself. She needed clear guidance to support the development of responsibility and in the development of her personal relationship with her peers.

Our primary aim as Lisa's teachers was to encourage her to gain a sense of self-control. She needed to learn about her behaviour and how it was affecting her peers and teachers. She also needed to gain self-esteem. We developed a programme to teach her to begin to understand and take charge of her behaviour and develop peer acceptance.

We had already developed a set of 'classroom rules' for all students. The teachers collaborated with the students to create a framework of common rules and responsibilities. The rules were compiled to simply explain fair and expected behaviours relevant to different situations and they were age appropriate for infants. In developing a personal plan with Lisa we went back to these rules as a basis for teaching patterns of new behaviour. We also linked her understanding about the rules directly to it.

By re-establishing these rules, Lisa began to understand that if she were to ignore them, then there would be necessary and fair consequences (such as time-out after any major tantrum, or the hurting of others).

These rules were compiled in picture form and used routinely throughout the day to encourage and remind all the children to use their classroom rules.

Lisa was further introduced to 'individual behaviour management plans', which proved to be a powerful and positive training and behaviour management tool.

The steps we took in establishing her plan included:

1   identifying (including 'mirroring', p. 31)
2   modelling
3   practising
4   encouraging
5   evaluating the behaviour (and celebrating her effort).

Mirroring

I asked Lisa if she would allow us to mirror the disruptive behaviour that she was frequently displaying. We were cautious of our tone of voice, making sure we were always supportive and inviting Lisa to join in at any time. She often laughed when we mirrored her typical disruptive behaviour.

We also took digital photographs of Lisa in her happier, positive moments and used these photographs as a cue; a reminder to encourage her in her 'happier' behaviours: 'Ask before you borrow'; 'Say excuse me when moving around others'; 'Sharing'; 'Positive language — "please", "thanks" ...'; 'See the teacher or the teaching assistant if you have a problem with work or another student instead of hitting out ...'

The pictures enabled Lisa to compare and contrast the wrong behaviour she was displaying with the right behaviour she should have been developing. Because a lot of her behaviour arose from frustration and anger, we were careful to point out (many times) that it was OK to be frustrated or angry, but that it was not alright to hurt others 'because you're angry'.

When discussing the plan with Lisa, we would ask her questions about her behaviour such as: 'What are you doing in the picture?'; 'How do you think the other children feel when you behave like this?'

Once the plan had been discussed, we modelled the new behaviour with Lisa and she would join in and practise them with us.

By taking these learning steps, Lisa was able to identify her new behaviour and see the positive outcomes.

Also, by giving Lisa specific feedback on her behaviours such as 'I like the way you are playing so nicely with Nathan', it encouraged Lisa to *continue behaving appropriately and to see that we were noticing her positive and responsible behaviours.*

Discipline
We avoided asking 'why' questions when we needed to remind and correct her about appropriate behaviour. Instead we used 'what', 'how' and 'when' questions. For example, 'What are you doing?'; 'What should you be doing now?'; 'What do you need to do — in your plan — if you are upset and angry?' This enabled Lisa to answer the questions about her behaviour directly. By giving Lisa clear instructions, she was able to understand exactly what she should be doing.

With perseverance, planning and ongoing support, Lisa was able to overcome her old pattern of frequent disruptive, stubborn and angry behaviour, and interact with the class in a manner respected by both her peers and teachers. We called the plan 'Lisa's happy chart' and kept daily records of behaviours that enabled happiness for herself (and her class peers) — in contrast to her 'old' frustration — stubborn — anger patterns of behaviour.

Since Lisa has been on the plan we have hardly had to use the time-out consequence.

The individual behaviour management plans proved to be a life-saver — there has been a huge turn around in Lisa's behaviour. I'm so proud of her but not as proud as she is of herself.

Sarah

Anger diaries

There are also a differences in the degree of frustration or anger that a person feels. Learning to be aware of those differences and what circumstances, situations and people lower one's tolerance to frustration is an important aspect of self-knowledge. A feeling thermometer or an anger diary can help measure this. Anger diaries can be a useful way of helping children (and teachers) to learn what situations or circumstances trigger their anger. When people become more aware of their anger arousal they are more likely to be able to manage it. If teachers can learn to recognise the triggers to children's anger they may be able to discern what is happening and then distract or divert in the short term. Appropriate use of humour, for example, can be a marvellous defuser in tense situations. I've always thought that the phrase 'I lost my temper' is imprecise — we *find* our 'temper' and subsequent anger. I have heard many young men (and children) say, 'I couldn't help it … I just lost my temper!' My response (at the right moment) is to remind them they found it (and when they've found their anger boy did they 'serve it up'!) There is often a wry smile from older children followed by the more difficult discussion about 'choosing our behaviour' (p. 124).

We can't choose our emotions but we can 'choose' our responses to those emotions; we can learn better and more constructive ways to communicate and manage our frustration.

Anger diaries can include a drawing of a thermometer that notes the degree of anger felt and what situations are causing it (degrees of mild or 'not very' through to 'I've blown it!' — out of control). Children need help with filling these in initially, they can also learn to use them in a self-directed way. With small children a picture diary with four stages of anger arousal shown can be used (see PM 18 in the appendix).

When working with children who suffer frustration or tolerance problems, I often use the word 'angries' (I point to my tummy and head) to describe the feeling of anger. Then I discuss what can be done when the 'angries' are there. This awareness assists the student in identifying the

feeling of frustration and the situations that make him angry. He might assume that the stares of others, or their refusals to play, mean he is 'no good', or that he is 'stupid' or they 'hate him'. The teacher can make it clear to the student that she does not dislike the student, but 'we' don't like these kinds of *behaviours* (be specific) that may also be causing others to 'reject' him.

These diaries can be used to discuss the anger triggers with the child (this is best done daily with children who display frequent anger outbursts). Initially, the teacher will need to fill it in *with* the student until he gets used to connecting situations with the pictures. In recovery sessions we can then discuss what we have noticed about his 'angries', where they come from, and what he can do about it.

Developing an anger management plan

While it is OK to be angry there are some behaviours (arising from poorly handled anger) that are unacceptable. These behaviours need to be explained clearly to the child. They include:

- throwing furniture or equipment
- pinching, punching or 'stabbing' with pencils
- elbowing, biting, regular 'stomping', kicking or spitting in temper
- regular use of verbal aggression and swearing at others.

Some *aspects* of these anger behaviours can even be mirrored (pp. 31–4). Verbal aggression can be overt (towards others or inanimate objects!) or covert (towards the self as maladaptive self-talk). Again, it is the frequency, intensity and duration of these behaviours that is the cause for concern. Behaviour recovery can teach alternatives to these actions so that children know that when they get angry they can do other (specifically planned and rehearsed) behaviours instead.

Of course it is the *characteristic* behaviour, not the isolated incident, that needs to be addressed. Not all the above behaviours stem from anger. They may arise from attention-seeking or trying to exercise power over others — children who try to show peers and the teacher that no one can make them behave! Kicking furniture, hitting out at others, screaming and throwing tantrums arc not acceptable. While teachers can understand that some children will deal with their emotions in this way it is important, for the rights of all, to set a safety context with limits, understanding of clear consequences and the teaching of alternatives.

It can be helpful if the teacher shares her own understanding of anger to help the student tune into his experiences. 'Have you noticed what happens when you get angry? When I get angry I sometimes close my fists like this. My neck goes stiff. I frown and I breathe funny.' A bit of mirroring can be helpful here. 'Have you noticed anything like that when you get angry? Can I tell you what I've noticed when you get angry?'

'I've noticed, Matthew, that you often get angry (show him the angry face on the diary) when you *can't* do the work (or whatever). I've noticed, too, that you clench your fists and breathe like this. Do you know I get angry too sometimes? I can understand how you feel that way. When I get angry my shoulders tense (model); my brows (see here) go in; my fists go tight (like this). But I've learned that *when I* get angry I can relax my neck muscles by doing this. I take four breaths. I relax my neck, my shoulders and back. I relax my fists and arms and my eyes. I also tell myself that I can relax, that it's not worth getting angry just because I can't do something or get something I want. After I've relaxed I try again, and I feel better.' This sharing helps build rapport. We can invite the child to make an anger plan. Invite him to practise simple 1, 2, 3 relaxation (see PM 12 in the appendix).

The language of choice

A central tenet of behavioural responsibility is the emphasis placed on choosing behaviour — both negative and positive in outcome. Children need to learn that they are making choices — no one is actually *making* them throw furniture, or scream, spit or kick. This is a difficult concept to convey, but an essential one. Once teachers accept and treat children as if they can't help being aggressive in this way, they do them a great disservice. They need to be treated on the basis that they are making choices. Even if the student refuses offers of assistance to understand his behaviour and make a plan, he still needs to be treated as if that is his 'choice'. Nor is he helped with threats — he is feeling those angry feelings. Denying it, or telling him to deny it, won't help. This is a difficult concept to learn — that there is a significant element of 'choice' in our behaviour.

When we remind the student that his behaviour is 'his choice' we need to do so in a supportive sense (not in any supercilious way). The teacher also reminds the student (in a calmer time) that she will help and support the student to make better choices about his behaviour for better outcomes.

Choosing behaviour means choosing consequences as well. Behavioural responsibility includes the ability to predict the consequences. Behaviour recovery includes teaching the child to think about, 'What will happen if and when … ?' The teacher will remind the student again that his behaviour is his 'choice'; we (as his teacher) can help him make better choices for better outcomes. It is important that the child be allowed to choose (his consequences) even if he says he 'doesn't care!' Letting him know, in advance, the consequences of his present aggressive behaviour will help. Consistency in the application of behaviour consequences, throughout the recovery process, is also essential.

Thinking and feeling

Older primary age children can be taught the relationship between thinking, feeling and behaviour. Angry or frustrated behaviour often relates to what is *characteristically* thought and believed (p. 57). Strong feelings of anger also relate to what people believe and say to themselves about situations and circumstances. This message can be taught to older children using recovery-type teaching approaches. Using cartoon-type pictures and some brief one-to-one mirroring, teachers illustrate and discuss how angry thoughts and angry self-talk can often make the student feel worse — especially if he *keeps* saying those angry things, or negative things, over and over (see PM 13 in the appendix).

One way to illustrate the link between thought, emotion and action is to mirror the self-talk aloud to the student while acting in an angry way. For example, the teacher will say aloud 'I can't stand it!' *while* throwing books on the floor, pushing furniture or slamming the door. If we suspect the child might be intimidated in any way by such mirroring, the teacher can *generalise* the behaviour by saying, 'Some children do this when they get angry', or by simply asking his permission. 'Can I show you what I mean? Can I show you what some children say inside their head when they get very angry?' or 'I'd like to show you ... OK?' The student is then shown how a different kind of self-talk can help him do better and feel better when he gets angry.

The recovery plans can focus on typical self-defeating speech and self-defeating behaviour such as, 'I hate this class!'; 'I can't stand it!'. It is useful to ask the child, 'Are these thoughts helping thoughts or thoughts that will make things worse', or 'What might happen if a person *keeps* thinking these kinds of thoughts each time something hard or unpleasant happens?' Everyone gets upset, annoyed, irritated, but how upset they become is affected by what they *normally* say inside their heads at the time they feel under pressure. This message — that emotions and the degree of stress felt is affected by beliefs as well as the event — is a difficult one for adults, let alone children (Bernard & Joyce 1984). What we are trying to teach the child is that he can learn to take some control over how bad he feels by learning to tune-in to his self-talk and use appropriate thought-stoppers. 'Hey the work is not dumb — it's just hard. I can do it with my plan.' Thought-stoppers can also help in self-prediction of consequences. 'If I keep saying this to myself, I'll feel worse — I might even end up in trouble.'

Modifying negative self-talk won't eliminate negative and bad feelings, but the child won't feel *as* bad about the situation. It is another tool that increases his sense of self-control. In the appendix there are some key picture cue plans to illustrate the link between self-talk (or self-guiding speech) and behaviour. These 'think bubbles' can be recorded as a visual *aide memoire;* older children can employ the iconic image of replacing a negative 'CD' message with a more positive and realistic internal 'CD' message (p. 69).

Distracting oneself within a stressful situation can be taught as a strategy for a child with low frustration tolerance: moving to another place to work in the classroom, doing an alternative task for a while, going to see a teacher on playground duty when feeling really frustrated or angry. One common self-distracting approach for older children is self-imposed time-out (SITO). The student 'contracts' with his teacher (or case supervisor at secondary level p. 25) to leave the room for five or ten minutes to sit in a safe place and cool down, and to do this only if he feels the

pressure 'to blow' is getting too strong. As part of a plan for anger ma.... ment the 'leaving' can be left to the student's discretionary ownership (not in instructional time). The viability of this approach needs to be discussed with colleagues and discarded if abused by the student. It has, however, been used very successfully by many teachers.

Teaching assertion behaviour to children is a common feature of social skills programmes. It is not only non-assertive children who need such skills; overly hostile or verbally aggressive children need to learn the difference between being aggressive and being assertive. This is where one-to-one modelling by the teacher is so powerful in clarifying the difference. By setting up common situations where assertive responses are appropriate and then practising the words and gestures, students can learn to observe social cues more carefully and not read aggression into every bump, encroachment of personal space or 'touchy' interpersonal responses.

One of the goals of behaviour recovery is the enhancement of the student's self-esteem *within his classroom group* by gaining peer acceptance. By teaching the student how to relate non-aggressively (so he doesn't punch the student who takes or 'steals' his pencil without asking), teachers are increasing the likelihood of peer approval and social belonging.

Because some children's aggressive behaviour is a badly focused (and habituated) way of belonging, it is important that the classroom group discusses how aggressive behaviour makes it feel. Many schools use classroom meetings as a forum in which students can learn to express their feelings and concerns in an open and assertive way, and also to learn how to solve problems, co-operate with and help one another, without resorting to aggression. When *characteristically* aggressive children hear their peers talking about behaviour they don't (and do) like, such peer disapproval can (in itself) have a salutary effect on understanding and moderation of behaviour. The teacher can then guide the discussion to work out solutions and propose skills sessions where students can learn to relate to one another without easy and quick recourse to unnecessary aggression.

It might also be added that such children will benefit from an adequate programme of physical activity within the school's curriculum. It allows for appropriate, normal and healthy energy expressions. Even brief morning exercise can be helpful to this end. Children will also benefit from relaxation activities built into a teaching day (this is most common at primary level). A very helpful resource for whole-class relaxation skills is Jenny Rickard's very practical and positive book, *Relaxation Activities For Children*, ACER Press (1994).

Bullies

Bullies are found in every age group (I have encountered 'colleagues' who bully others) and they learn early that their behaviour gets them what they want. Like aggression, bullying is a learned behaviour (Besag 1989).

Bullies accept hostility and aggression as part of their world and use such means to gain their sense of belonging or peer popularity, to maintain group leadership and influence others by threat to act, or relate to them in a way that satisfies their quest for 'relational power'. Most bullying in schools is psychological bullying, but it is nonetheless distressing for those who are victims of such behaviour. Children who bully are less empathetic to the feelings of others (Smith & Thompson 1991) and have little affectional monitoring of their own behaviour. They may be limited in their moral reasoning, believing that it is the likelihood of punishment that determines any 'wrongness' in their behaviour. The crime is in being caught, not how their behaviour is affecting the rights and needs of others. Indeed, this is the hardest truth to get through to bullies; in their distorted idiosyncratic logic they often believe their victims deserve to 'get done' because of the way they look, act, talk and behave ('It serves them right').

Bullying is forcing others to do, act and feel the very things a bully would never want done to him. Bullying is not accidental, it is a learned behaviour.

Bullying means:

• courage	→ translates as	→ coercion
• personal fear	→ is directed into	→ others being frightened
• anger	→ is replaced by	→ aggression
• personal inadequacy	→ is transferred into	→ an abuse of power
• fun	→ is replaced by	→ hurting others for pleasure
• personal suffering	→ is transferred	→ into causing others suffering
• a bully's game	→ becomes	→ a nightmare for the victim
• power	→ is	→ abused

The victims:

- are smaller, weaker, different (in looks, speech, background, friendship, strength)

- are less able (or unable) to directly, assert their rights or defend themselves
- may have low self-esteem or lack social confidence
- sometimes are likely not to tell or do anything except confirm the bully's 'world view'. (An abuse of relational power gets you what you want.) If a victim believes that reporting means he may not be believed or that nothing effectively will be done to stop the bullying, he may continue unnecessarily suffering as a victim.

There needs to be clear, school-wide consequences for bullying behaviour. Without clear consequences for such behaviour the bully continues in his (learned) belief that he can get his own way with impunity (Olweus 1978). Such consequences need to be set within a due process for dealing with bullying behaviour and an *educational* and policy context that emphasises rights-respecting behaviour. These consequences will be:

- known in advance and published in a school-wide policy document
- explained to all students in relation to what the school means by bullying
- discussed within classroom meeting time, during the establishment phase of the year, and at times when the school experiences any spate of bullying behaviour.

The normal features of consequences also apply; particular behaviour leads to *certain*, and clear, consequences. This is hard. My own feeling about bullies has often been, 'I'd like to give them the same as they give to ...' This action would briefly ameliorate my strong feelings, no doubt, but merely confirm the student's warped world view. It is the fair, *known* certainty of a consequential process that will 'carry the day', not the tempting severity applied by the teacher.

Like any use of consequences on serious behavioural issues, planning and policy direction needs to be established on a whole-school basis.

Dealing with bullies

It is important to have a due process for dealing with bullies that is consistent with the school's policy on behaviour management. This due process needs to embrace both consequences and, where possible, some form of behaviour recovery.

- Isolate the bully for a formal meeting with a senior teacher. If there are several bullies within a collusive group it is better to deal with them one by one.

- It should be explained to the student(s) what is known about the bullying: 'I need to talk to you because I've heard (or know) you've been saying (or doing) to …' Name the victim and be as specific as possible about the bullying behaviour (Pikas 1991).

- The ideal situation, of course, is where there is direct knowledge of the bullying behaviour; often the knowledge is 'second-hand' or (sometimes) from the victim. It is also important to check the bully's version of events: 'What do you know about this?' (again be as specific as possible). 'What has been happening?' Encourage the bully to talk about it. This is not always easy. Where there is no direct knowledge, it is important to avoid rushing the dialogue or using open interrogatives. 'Why did you do it?' Closed interrogatives are more effective. ('This is

what we know about the bullying. We want to know what happened?'; 'What did you say?'; 'How many times?'; 'When?'; 'Where?')

- The bullying student is asked, 'How the victim (name) might feel when
  …' Mirroring the bullying behaviour can often establish some visual
  and emotional rapport, clarifying to the bully what his bullying behaviour looks and 'feels' like. Encouraging empathy and perspective-taking
  of others' situation and circumstances is always a challenge when
  working with children who bully. Classroom meetings, victim — perpetrator mediation (p. 138) and whole-school educational emphasis
  will all assist empathetic thinking.
- Reference should be made to the school's rules about safety and
  respect, and the consequences of behaving in ways that hurt others'
  rights. It needs to be explained again what it means to bully others
  and why it is wrong and totally unacceptable. It is not 'a joke'; it is not
  'fun', even if some others 'do stuff like this'. If the bullying is physical,
  involving other students, we can use the term assault and explain how
  people can be 'charged with assault'. Older students can be shown the
  school policy.
- Make a plan to address bullying behaviour reframed as 'safe' and 'fair'
  behaviour. Any plan needs to gain the bully's agreement about stopping all such behaviour. The student will be encouraged to come up
  with a positive plan: 'What can you do to fix up your behaviour?
  What will you do so that (name victim) can feel safe now?'

If there has *previously* been a class meeting where the peer ethos is
clearly against bullying, the teacher should explain, yet again to the bullying student, what his peers think about this kind of behaviour. ('What
are some other ways we can be noticed, feel good in the group and enjoy
having friends?') The difference between aggression and assertion can also
be modelled and explained. ('What does it mean to legitimately stand-up
for yourself without hurting others and on purpose?')

Any plan needs to be simple, and directed at the student's level of
understanding. Explain why persistent name-calling, teasing, threats,
racist language or physical hurting is wrong. No one *deserves* this. It is
wrong and it must stop. If the student whinges about not liking 'x', 'y' or
'z', point out that while he does not have to like 'x', 'y' or 'z', he does have
to respect them. Give some examples of basic respect: 'Excuse me' instead
of pushing in, using a fellow student's name instead of a nasty put-down
name, asking to join in a game, or borrow a bat or ball instead of barging
in, spoiling or snatching.

It may be necessary for physically aggressive bullies to be isolated
from social play for a period of time and have their playtime while others

are inside. This means the bully still enjoys his right to playtime, but is isolated from his peers, with a teacher as a minder. It may also be necessary to have staggered home times for bullies if there is clear evidence of them threatening, extorting or engaging in aggressive behaviour on the way to or from school. These approaches should be:

- explained to the parent(s)
- explained as a related consequence, not merely as a punishment, and be part of a counselling/contracting process
- designed to teach a connection between behaviour and outcome.

Bullies and relational power

Most children will quarrel, argue, challenge or even hit out, on occasion, at others when angry. They will exhibit these behaviours because of frustration, tiredness, crowded conditions, developmental considerations, provocation and so on. These behaviours are not bullying. Bullying is selective, intentional, often secretive (accompanied by threats) and repetitive. Bullying can be psychological (teasing, racist or sexist slurs and accusations, put-downs, threats to do something) or physical and is sometimes both. Boys are much more likely to use physical bullying.

Bullies are characterised by their abuse of relational power. All bullying is an exercise in power and control to the degree in which it satisfies the need to feel important and significant. Students who frequently and disturbingly display patterns of bullying behaviour often come from dysfunctional families and have been bullied themselves. A significant number go on to display traits of delinquency and to an engagement with the criminal justice system (four times more likely to do so according to a study by Eron 1987).

Everyone has some degree of relational power. Bullying is more than a misuse of this power (it is that); bullies abuse the exercise of power *socially*. While such behaviour is always present and observed with monotonous regularity in politics, films and sitcoms, playgrounds, families, between nations, it cannot be excused on that basis. One of the factors likely to perpetuate bullying in schools is the attitudes that endorse it. Bullying is wrong (even if 'always with us') because it acts against the fundamental right of students to feel safe at school. Bullying is also perpetuated by the code of silence about such behaviour where students believe that to tell is to 'dob' or to 'tell tales' (pp. 134–5)

Bullies trade in 'secrecy' (not from the school peers to whom their social power is directed) from adults. Cracking the 'secrecy code' is crucial in addressing any kind of bullying.

A whole-school approach

Smith and Thompson (1991) in their research on bullying have outlined features and characteristics of 'low-bullying' and 'high-bullying' schools. The most significant factor in distinguishing between the two is the degree to which teachers and administrators have firmly held views about the unacceptability of bullying and have a whole-school policy in place to address it. This policy should involve all staff, students and parents wherever possible. Other features of low-bullying schools include the degree to which victims are taken seriously, listened to, allowed to tell their story without the brush-off, and the certainty that due process will follow bullying incidents. For example, in the playground where most bullying occurs (because it's harder to be seen) victims should always be listened to ('I'm glad you felt you could tell me') and then a follow-up process organised with the class teacher.

The school's educational programme should address protective behaviours and what it means to enjoy the right to feel safe. For example, rather than merely having an anti-bullying programme, it is more effective to develop a positive behaviour programme *within which* bullying behaviour is addressed. What are the behaviour management practices of staff — generally speaking?

Is there a correlation between bullying (verbal bullying) by teaching staff and the tacit acceptance by children of such behaviour? If there are teachers who utilise public shaming, undue (and persistent) criticism, put-downs, intentional embarrassment and sarcasm, aggressive (rather than assertive) management styles, then such adult modelling will clearly have an effect and easily override any policy statement about self-discipline and respect for mutual rights!

School policy

School policy should outline what bullying is, the due process taken when bullying is reported, how victims and bullies are treated, contact procedures with parents, and the educational overlap with the school's rights, responsibilities, rules and consequences. The school can address bullying in a range of ways:

1   Education can raise awareness of what bullying is, how people feel when it happens and what can be done about it. Drama, role-playing, story-telling and classroom meetings are ideal vehicles for exploring the issues at stake. Both bullies and victims can see themselves as

others see them and hear what their peers believe needs to be done. Education is especially important in creating an environment which accepts that 'It's OK to tell if someone keeps on doing ...' Classroom meetings can explore how this reporting can be done confidently. The student community can increase the sense of social security when it collectively views bullying as wrong.

An extremely helpful book for infant children — addressing realistic bullies and victims — is the picture story book *No More Bullying!* by Rosemary Stones (1991). This book provides a 'typical' bullying behaviour story among girls, although its message is relevant at any age, infant to lower primary. It also illustrates how parents might perceive bullying. Its strength lies in the totally realistic characterisation and behaviour of 'victim', 'bully' and 'audience of peers' (including collusive bullies). It is published by Dinosaur Publications (a Harper-Collins imprint).

2 It is important to establish a due process for assisting victims and addressing bullies.

3 Clear consequences for bullying need to be outlined to the students. These can include isolation, partial withdrawal from playtimes, supervision and in some cases temporary exclusion from school.

4 Contact with parents is crucial, but the school will need to outline how it will do this in a non-judgemental and supportive way. Having a clear policy, with a published due process, will help the communication between home and school.

5 'Safe areas' at playtimes (library, art room, alternative programmes) need to be created — not all students want highly active play.

6 Peer arbitrator programmes can assist in a climate of 'relaxed vigilance' about safe and fair play and recreation. A child can go to a peer arbitrator trained in mediating (they normally wear a badge or hat, or are well known to all students).

7 Bullies need to learn to behave differently; *teaching* behaviour change on a one-to-one basis can help develop these skills. Victims of bullying behaviour can also be assisted with recovery options. These will emphasise social confidence and assertive behaviour.

Peer involvement

One of the schools I worked in had signs up for a while, of a bully face with a 'no' line through it and the acronym DOB. It had a two-way meaning: 'Don't obey bullies' and 'Dob on a bully' (tell teachers about bullying when and where it is happening). It proved most successful. They also held a number of classroom meetings across the school to deal with the Australian cringe about 'dobbing' (tale-telling), wanting to get someone else into trouble, or paying them back or getting lots of attention from the teacher or other students. *Asking for help or support from the teacher is not dobbing*; letting a teacher know when several students are ganging up on others, or threatening them, or using racist put-downs repeatedly to taunt is not dobbing; letting a teacher know when the threat merchants are abusing toilet privileges is not dobbing — *it's putting those who can help in the know*; that is, adults who can support and make the bullying stop. Classroom meetings, with a consideration of specific questions, are a positive vehicle for clarifying this issue with children. 'How does this behaviour affect you directly? In what way does it work against others' rights? What can we do?' (See p. 88.)

Protective behaviour programmes have taught children that, 'Nothing is so bad that we can't tell'; 'Nothing is so bad that something can't be done about it'. Teachers need to be careful not to lightly dismiss reports by victims or observers. If we suspect that a victim or the observers are 'ambiguous', or out for revenge, then we will need to check with our colleagues to get a rounded picture. However, children should always be encouraged to report if the bullying doesn't stop.

Helping victims

I have worked with many adults in the workplace who have recounted being bullied. They felt (and believed) that they were powerless to do anything. Worse it was 'somehow their fault'. At school, victims (unless they are the 'bully-turned-victim') tend to be reluctant to tell. They may display low self-esteem in terms of successful adaption to the social world. (A person can be a loner and still be successful in terms of social adaption.) Loners who are 'victims' tend to play alone, have limited and poor social network skills, and exhibit an unhappiness (exacerbated by poor social networking) and a lack of positive friendships network.

When a student reports being bullied it is crucial that teachers take him seriously. He should be encouraged to talk about what has happened, and receive the support of reliable student observers. It is also important that teacher listening and interviewing remain calm and careful. Teachers should not over-react. They should let the child tell his story with supportive prompting.

When? Where? How? Whom? How often? This is the hardest part; encourage the student to talk and give a clear picture. If students do not report bullying, yet the teachers believe bullying is occurring, it will be necessary to carefully broach our concerns, directly, to the student. 'It's OK to talk about it if it ever happens to you.' As with all one-to-one sessions, ethical probity is essential, especially with male teachers and female victims. The safest approach is to raise the issue of suspected 'silent victims' with colleagues and plan a meeting with the child based on colleague advice and policy guidelines.

Bullying may be occurring when students regularly complain of losing things or of missing belongings. They may have bruises they won't talk about, or don't want to go out at lunch-time or recess. Is the child overly withdrawn? Frequently complaining of pains (headaches, stomach aches)? Has the student lost interest in school work? These observations should not be lightly dismissed, especially when reported by parents. The ideal situation is to work with the parents to develop and encourage the child to talk it out and develop appropriate support and follow appropriate due process.

Strategies for victims

Victims of bullying need reassurance, they want to be believed and supported. Most of all they want the bullying to stop. Encouraging them to report what is happening and who is doing it can enable teachers to then work with the bully/bullies as well. The following strategies are used widely in schools, often in combination. As well as stopping and confronting the bullying in a particular instance, teachers may need to teach the victim strategies for dealing with bullies wherever they are. Teachers, or other adults, will not always be around.

1   Children should be encouraged to play with others rather than alone. One primary school used a classroom meeting approach to raise the issue of children having and complaining of no one to play with. Two classes held concurrent meetings to discuss ways of making sure 'we all had someone to play with'. The most novel suggestion was that anyone who didn't have someone to play with should sit on the seats underneath the flagpole in the playground. If anyone was sitting there someone from one of the classes would go up and invite them to play. It worked. They called it their 'friendship seat'.

2   A peer-minder can be employed for a while to play with the victim in the playground along the lines of the plan helper idea (see p. 76).

3   If a bully threatens a child, the potential victim can say straight away that 'Mr/Mrs knows about what you've been doing and saying. If you touch me (or my bag, my food, my bike) I'll report it'. This, at least,

lets the bully know that adults are aware of what is happening. They may think twice and weigh up the consequences. Some bullying occurs on the way to and from school, and bullies need to know that this behaviour (even in non-school contexts) will always be followed up. It is also important for teachers to realise that persistent 'minor' harassment (taking property without asking or giving back, kicking someone else's schoolbag around) is very stressful. It is important to deal with this at the classroom and duty-of-care level (wet-day supervision, playground). If staff are seen to give up their time and get to the facts and take action, as fairly as possible, students are more likely to report, feel supported, and also believe that support is available in more major aspects of bullying (Smith & Thompson 1991). Teachers need to be *relaxedly* vigilant about so-called 'minor' harassment.

4   All teachers should follow through and report bullying incidents wherever they occur in the school. Even those victims who are bullies and become prey to others who are stronger need support and guidance rather than a mere, 'It serves you right'.

5   Classroom meetings connected with themes such as being safe in the playground and bullying can be conducted. Children can discuss the following questions:

- What do we mean by bullying?
- What sort of people bully others?
- Where does it normally occur?
- Why do you think people bully others?
- What do they get out of it? How can we stop bullying?
- What sort of things would be helpful to say?
- What should we do if we see bullying happening?
- How can we support someone we know or see who is being bullied?
- How could we report bullying?
- What should happen to bullies?

These meetings can also discuss the difference between what students should do to reasonably handle themselves when hassled, how they can work co-operatively to settle differences, and how to report to teachers when it's getting too much. Students need to balance the difficult realities that there won't always be a teacher there, or an adult, when they're being hassled, teased, put down, threatened, excluded, or even hurt by bullies; and they have a right to feel safe, be treated with respect, and to know it's OK to report.

6   A skills programme can be organised across the school that focuses on the difference between students standing up for their rights to feel safe (and be treated with respect) and learning to handle the bullies of this world with confidence. Indeed, confidence is as much a skill as a state of mind. Students with low self-esteem can be encouraged to undertake activities that will increase their risk-taking, such as interviewing others for a project or speaking in front of the class (Borba & Borba 1982; Cranfield & Wells 1976; McGrath & Francey 1993).

7   If the victim is willing it can be useful to arrange a formal meeting where the victim has a supported opportunity to confront the bully with his behaviour. The meeting is planned ahead by the adult facilitator and the victim to discuss what issues to raise, and how. The victim explains to the bully what it is he is doing and that he wants the bullying to stop. The effect that such bullying has should be described briefly. The bully then has to agree it will stop and be specific about what he will do.

It is important that the tone of such a meeting be calm and positive, without denying the seriousness of such behaviours. Key questions can be asked.

- What happened?
- Why do you think it happened (or has been going on)?
- What rule or right is affected?
- What can we (you) do to stop it?

It is also important at such a meeting that the facilitator encourage the bully (bullies) to answer the questions in their own words. If the bullying is concerned with physical aggression, or threats of the same, the bully needs to be reminded that this is assault and it is very serious. The consequences for such behaviour will need to be spelled out. Of course, this process can be carried out with the victim and bully (bullies) separately, but there is value (if the victim is confident enough) in addressing the bully face-to-face with teacher support. If these meetings are held separately it can still be useful to get the bully and victim together, so that the victim can hear the bully say that his behaviour will stop.

It is better to deal with collusive bullies separately (one-to-one) from the main perpetrator of the bullying. If a meeting is conducted with a group of bullies they tend to discount their behaviour.

Teaching assertion

Assertion is first and foremost a skill. It is a way of making a person's needs and rights known without trampling on the rights of others. It is a skill needed by both the bully and the victim. Using the programme approach outlined in Chapter 3 the class teacher (or support teacher) can set up one-to-one or small-group teaching sessions to outline the need for this skill, practising the skills (using role-play similar to the setting in which it will be needed), and getting feedback from the student as they use such skills in a 'natural setting'.

While bullying is never right, there are some victims whose interpersonal behaviours may unfortunately highlight behaviours that bullies disturbingly seem to pick on:

- being a loner, playing alone
- a characteristic whine in the voice
- lowered hang-dog look
- non-confident body posture
- hunched-over shoulders
- skewed, darting, uncertain eye-contact
- hands hung low, passive stance.

Children who look like this do not look as if they are 'in control'. While this is not their fault, it presents an unfortunate picture to the child's peers. The sad reality is that they are more likely to be picked on than other students. If recovery meetings are set up to support victims the teacher will explain that: 'When people pick on you, or tease ... there won't always be others there to help, so I want to show you a plan that will help you.' Using gentle mirroring techniques the teacher can model the sorts of behaviours above and ask the student, 'What do you think others feel when we look (here the teacher models) and speak like this?' The student is then encouraged to look at other kinds of behaviours:

1   The teacher helps the student understand how he presents to others. 'What does your behaviour look like, sound like? Do you know?' He may not be aware of how he typically 'comes across' to others.

2   The teacher explains to the child that when he 'takes charge', he can learn to speak and behave and feel differently; stronger and without so much fear.

3   A scenario is discussed similar to the situation the child experiences using picture cues and modelling techniques. The teacher then models new assertive behaviours.

4   Student and teacher practise the new assertive behaviours and play/reaction suggestions. Such teaching sessions need to be spaced out over time to avoid 'overload'.

Positive ignoring

Teachers can discuss and model 'positive ignoring' behaviours; it's OK to walk away (walk tall) from teasing and name-calling. It's a good idea, though, to encourage the student to walk away towards a teacher or to some students with whom he feels safe. In the one-to-one sessions the student is encouraged to practise walking tall and walking away while the simulated teasing is going on. Positive ignoring strategies can be used: 'The names can't really hurt me unless I believe they can. Inside my head I am still OK'. Teachers often set up such assertive learning skills in paired learning with a highly supportive and responsible student working with the victim of bullying. Part of each teaching session can also address self-talk (see p. 57).

It can be useful to make up a practice card for this self-talk (see PM 16a and 16b in the appendix). If the parents are supportive this can be practised at home as well as at school. The next time a student says or does the bullying behaviour the child can:

- turn and face the bully
- look into his eyes
- speak into his eyes
- stand tall, head up without smiling
- tell the bully what it is he doesn't like without shouting or arguing, and finish with a 'stop' statement
- walk away, towards other students or the teacher.

If, in rehearsal time, the student still adopts a non-assertive, whining voice, it will be important to give feedback and 'coach' the skill: 'Listen carefully and watch me.' (The teacher re-models the whole sequence.) 'Now, have another go.' Encourage any approximation towards the desired behaviour. It will take several goes before the new behaviour begins to connect in any meaningful way. It can help to practise it 'out of simulation' first, just like rehearsing a line in a play. Then practise it in a *simulated*, face-to-face setting. The teacher will also ask the student if he would like to practise this plan with a friend next time (a plan helper). These assertions and confidence skills will take some time; children develop these postural, tonal behaviours and non-assertive beliefs over a period of time. It will (like any other skill) take practice, effort, feedback and some real-time success.

Some victims of bullying are themselves ambiguous when it comes to uninvited teasing, name-calling or getting hit. They tease others, pick on them, 'stir' and hassle until they get a response (even being hit), then cry 'foul' to a teacher. It happens in classrooms from time to time and it is often a form of attention-seeking for the victim.

- It is important to avoid over-servicing the suspected victim. Stay calm, listen and focus on the problem.
- The victim is asked what happened and what he could do in a similar situation next time. If he doesn't know, he is given a plan that minimises adult intervention.
- If the teacher is certain that this victim is a 'teaser-cum-victim' it will help to explain to the student that if he keeps getting hassled all he has to do is keep doing what he's doing.

If bullying is going to be addressed effectively it will require a whole-school approach that includes attitude change, policy direction, positive management practices, a targeted education emphasis, adequate support for victims, and behaviour recovery for *both* victims and bullies.

Challenges of the Programme

8

No programme in itself, will solve the variety of problems presented by human behaviour within a school. Behaviour recovery is an attempt to bring some balance to the rights and responsibilities of the student with challenging behaviour and behaviour disorders. Consequently, the programme is also supportive of teachers and their rights and responsibilities. Like many programmes it uses bits of paper to help structure complicated reality: picture cues, diagrams, memory aids and checklists. However, at the end of any piece of paper is a human being. It is the human *relationship* within which the difficult task of teaching new behaviour occurs that really matters. This relationship is tested, frequently, in any journey of behaviour recovery and, inevitably, there are particular challenges and problem areas that need to be recognised and addressed.

Teachers have to create a safe, rights-enhancing environment for all students; an environment that can increase the students' opportunities for success at school and beyond. It is important to recognise that while the school cannot compensate for this student's home background there is a lot a school can do to increase a student's behaviour choices.

Some teachers will complain about being involved in programmes like behaviour recovery. 'Why should we spend all this time on one pain of a student!'; 'Why should I give up my time to cover another teacher's class so that a particularly troublesome student can have one-to-one attention?' These students, however, do have rights and needs, and yes they will have to face the consequences of their disruptive behaviour *as they should*. However, they do have needs that recovery support can meet. This is a whole-school effort — to support the class teacher and students and their families.

It needs to be affirmed that students who are supported in such programmes are not 'getting away with anything'. The school is simply setting up a positive colleague support structure, and providing a targeted programme to teach the student appropriate behaviours to enhance his learning and peer relationships. These students face the same corrective discipline as all students.

The programme has less likelihood of success if teachers do not give colleague support in covering classes (for one-to-one recovery time), time-out, rotation of the student on bad days and convey general good-will.

Where there appears to be a large number of 'difficult' students, as well as students with behaviour disorders (say up to 10 per cent of the class), teachers can:

- identify the most disturbing student(s) in the group and concentrate on them first
- work with students in pairs
- use a class-group reinforcement programme where the class is divided into mixed ability groups and 'reward' schedules developed to enhance on-task social/academic behaviours (see Rogers 1998, Chapter 7).

There is a percentage of students who resist all attempts to be assisted in behaviour change. If that resistance, over time, is significantly affecting the rights of the other students (and the teacher), then a formal inquiry and due processes will be needed to consider referral options outside the school. This should be urged by the administration on advice of the class teacher in consultation with specialist teachers.

Colleague support

The rationale for the specific teaching of positive behaviour at the level of time required by behaviour recovery-type models needs to be explained to all staff, especially specialist staff. The discipline protocols and practices will need to be clarified so a *consistency of practice is* more likely across all staff (see Chapter 6). There are a number of crucial areas which must be considered:

- The fundamental philosophy of the recovery model should be outlined (at a staff meeting or as the need arises). Particular plans for particular children should also be introduced to all staff as circumstances seem fit. This is essential if a student is on a recovery plan for playground behaviour.

- All specialist teachers should have a copy of any behaviour plans in use by the class teacher.
- An agreed use of 'cool-off time', exit (especially the procedural aspects) and time-out measures should be decided on. Who is involved for supported exit? Who are the colleagues one can call on? How? Where does the student go *during* time out? (See pp. 106.)

Specialist teachers need to be fully aware of the class teacher's normative discipline practices — even some key discipline language can be helpful. Reasonable consistency of discipline practice will assist the success of ongoing recovery options. It is advisable that consequences for disruptive behaviour in specialist time (or playtime) be normally carried out by the duty-of-care teacher at that time. Even if deferred consequences are used, the certainty-of-consequence principle is more likely to be realised (in the students' thinking) if the duty-of-care teacher follows through with the necessary (related) consequence.

Working with parents

Any school working with challenging and disordered student behaviour will often be in contact with parents. These 'meetings' should be as supportive as possible. Most parents will recognise that the school is doing its best and their support will be gained by school staff being non-judgemental about their parent role. Parental understanding and support for what is being done at school is very important.

There are some children whose disruptive behaviour patterns present from significant emotional pathology: trauma associated with family breakdown, emotional deprivation and anxiety about what is happening in the family (including abuse). Any suspicion of such preconditions affecting school behaviour needs to be dealt with through a team approach and specialist communication support extended to the family.

When explaining behaviour recovery to parents it is important to stress the supportive nature of the programme. Parents are not asked their permission for one-to-one withdrawal in class time, rather it is explained to them why this school programme will help their child work more positively in class, enable him to perform better in his work and help him feel better about himself as a person. The focus should be on the positive aspects of the programme without minimising the disruptive nature of their child's behaviour. It is explained that this approach is used in many schools to

enable students to recognise why their behaviour is a problem, and what they can do to learn positive behaviours.

Parents are shown the recovery teaching cards and teachers explain what is entailed in one-to-one sessions. Teachers will also discuss the possibility of utilising a classroom meeting approach (see Chapter 5), emphasising that classroom meetings are the regular forum whereby the class can raise issues of concern and work on a plan of action within the fair rules.

Time-out provisions need to be carefully explained *within the school's overall discipline policy*. When the child (any child, not just theirs!) makes it difficult for others to learn, feel safe or be treated with respect then he will have to face time-out consequences. The teacher will always clarify the difference between punishment and consequence with respect to time-out. Throughout parental discussions the teacher will emphasise the *educational* features of the programme and the goals of enhancing co-operative behaviours in (and out of) the classroom.

Occasional meetings with parents can provide opportunities for feedback and progress in the student's plan (and resulting behaviour). The monitoring cards are a useful aid here. The student can also be invited to these meetings. At one school (where parents were often rung up about their offspring's disruptive behaviour) the class teacher started to ring up about the positive behaviours following recovery support. Initially she got the following reply. '_____ (expletive)! What's he done now?'; 'Well Mrs _____, I just rang to say Damien's been working really well in maths today, especially ...' Silence. Then a more measured, 'Oh, yes, well, thank you for calling'. Damien came to school next day. 'Hey, what did you say to my mum yesterday?' 'Why?' 'Well she was a bit happy about what you said.' Few parents object to the attempts by a school to assist their children with behaviour recovery. Some parents even take the ideas and apply them in the home environment.

If the parents are generally hostile to school, to 'authority figures', a due process should be set up that protects the class teacher from unauthorised visits. No parents (thankfully it is few) have a right to barge into a school and verbally abuse and threaten staff. These parents will be formally advised of the school's discipline policy and why behaviour recovery approaches are being used. They are given a summary of what the programme is, in writing, and a copy of the school's discipline code. None of this, of course, can be carried out until a meeting can be arranged and parental misconception addressed. At any such meeting where parents become overly challenging or hostile, senior staff will need to be assertive and supportive, keeping the focus of any such meeting on the school's policy, support offered and *behaviour* addressed.

If the programme is clearly not working and significantly disruptive behaviour is normative, and parents continue to be unsupportive, the school will need to use sanctions such as suspension and pursue formal education department inquiry procedures.

The class teacher

The unique relationship that primary school teachers have with their students means that they are the ideal people to engage the child in the learning of new behaviours. While a 'behaviour tutor' can quite comfortably utilise the tenets of teaching behaviour, the fact that a tutor does not spend (normally speaking) significant day-in, day-out time with a child may work against the frequent encouragement essential to any success. Furthermore, the link between modelling and rehearsal and what happens in the classroom is not as strong when a tutor is involved. So, wherever possible, support should be given to the class teacher to engage in a teaching behaviour programme. There are some teachers who do not have (or cannot sustain) the emotional reserves necessary for one-to-one recovery support. There are teachers who may have a poor working relationship with the child in need of such a programme. In these cases another colleague is a more appropriate option for developing a Behaviour Recovery programme with the student.

The support colleague will act as *behaviour recovery tutor* and spend some time with the teacher in the classroom observing the child in the natural setting and building a working relationship prior to any recovery sessions.

Behaviour tutors

A 'behaviour tutor' can both assist and support the classroom teacher to regain a sense of proportion and possibility of change for the child in question. Such support (when it breeds any successful change in the child's behaviour) may rekindle enthusiasm and professional goodwill in the class teacher.

A tutor can develop the programme in the same way as the class teacher would, as long as it is someone reasonably well-known to the class: someone who has spent enough time with the students to be accepted as 'staff'. It can be a parent who is involved in learning support, a support teacher or school psychologist. What is crucial is that they are familiar with the programme of teaching behaviour (as outlined in this text) and have available the one-to-one time necessary for the programme.

It goes without saying that anybody selected to tutor the child does so within a team approach, and that he or she works effectively with the class teacher. Part of their role is to increase the congruence between success in one-to-one sessions with the student and how the class teacher can build on the rehearsal of target behaviours back in the natural setting of the classroom. Such tutors need to demonstrate enthusiasm; even a sense of humour; the ability to communicate well and give positive feedback; a non-judgemental stance; willingness to 'hang in there' so they can spot even the small approximations made by the child towards positive behaviour. While this sounds like a lot to ask, these are skills and professional attitudes possessed by any effective teacher.

There also needs to be an agreement between the class teacher, administration support and the tutor as to how the tutor time fits in with an overall plan to assist the class teacher and the student. Of particular importance is the release time from class and how it will be organised. Protocols for releasing the child from class need to be clarified and an agreement made that the class teacher will be supportive of the programme itself, each individual plan within the programme, and the feedback necessary by the class teacher to encourage the student in his progress with behaviour recovery. This needs to be clarified from the outset. It is counterproductive if the class teacher does not follow up what the tutor has been doing in his or her work with the student. This is crucial at secondary level in the relationship between case-supervisor and subject teachers (p. 25) Especially important is the frequent encouragement of positive behaviour, and approximations, by the student, to 'his plan'. It can be helpful if the tutor comes into the classroom on some occasions to model the quiet, often brief, encouragement essential to behaviour recovery plans (pp. 71–3).

The class teacher, or tutor, and supervising teacher also need to clarify the discipline procedures used: non-punitive in style, simple brief reminders or directions using the plan as a focus, choices instead of threats and planned, related consequences known in advance. It will need to be emphasised that the student with behaviour needs is not getting 'different discipline' (it is fundamentally the same as for all students), he is getting support outside the room to increase on-task and positive social behaviour within the classroom setting.

It is essential that the class teacher is not made to feel she is ineffective because a tutor is working with her. It is helpful, initially, if a supportive senior teacher can set up the teaming necessary to make the behaviour recovery initiative work. The emphasis ought to be that this is a whole-school, collegial, initiative to enable students with behaviour/ learning needs. This programme is used to give direct support to the classroom teacher (it does not diminish her professionalism). The class group, too, is supported when the school takes seriously the *structured* support of students with behaviour needs. Part of the tutor's role ought to be to work with the class teacher in the classroom — as much as time release allows. It can be useful for the tutor to support the class teacher in conducting at least one classroom meeting (see Chapter 5) to focus on what the class can do about disruptive behaviour.

Training of tutors should involve:

- familiarity with the Behaviour Recovery programme material
- assistance in preparation of picture cue material (see the appendix)
- regular evaluation of each recovery session with a senior supervising teacher and discussion with the classroom teacher (following one-to-one sessions with the student)
- discussion of the programme with any other teachers (inside or outside the school) using recovery approaches for teaching behaviour — particularly specialist teachers.

- understanding and use of time-out procedures (It will be necessary to clarify the use of time-out, in and out of the room, and how it can be utilised calmly and decisively.)
- how evaluation processes will be undertaken with the classroom teacher, tutor and senior staff.

Staying power

Children who have patterns of challenging and disordered behaviour will have heard many negative or mixed messages, resulting from their frustrating behaviour. 'What's wrong with you, how many times have I told you not to call out in class?'; 'Why can't you put your hand up like everyone else?'; 'No, you can't do your painting now because you haven't cleaned up your play dough mess yet, and I'm tired of telling you! When you leave the play dough out it gets hard and when it gets hard we can't use it, can we!' Negative messages, 'I'm sick of telling you!', interspersed with sarcasm or labelling ('idiot', 'stupid' or 'dumb') all have a self-fulfilling effect. Most of these kinds of messages and labels are the result of teacher frustration; natural frustration over a child's lazy, rude and indigent challenging behaviour.

It takes staying power to encourage these children towards responsible behaviours, appropriate social belonging and increased self-esteem. As Downing (1986) wrote, one needs to 'see the potential in this child'. A combination of behaviour recovery, positive discipline, active encouragement, and colleague support will help to attain this goal.

Defining success

It is important to consider what constitutes the success of a programme like behaviour recovery. Success can be described as a decrease in frequency, intensity and duration of disruptive behaviours with a corresponding increase in the on-task behaviours as developed with the programme. I've worked with teachers who complain that, 'He *still* calls out when we're having story time.'; 'He *still* rocks in his seat.'; 'He *still* calls out for help in instruction time.' It is important to ask, 'How many times now (since intervention) is he calling out, butting in or seat-wandering?' A drop in the frequency of distracting and disruptive behaviour — hopefully a significant drop — has to be seen as a success. Some teachers think that all disruptive behaviour should cease in order to prove any success for an intervention programme. This is clearly less than realistic; even 'well-behaved children' are disruptive from time to time (or at least distracting).

Remember, too, that any child in behaviour recovery is not given ɔ⊦ licence to be disruptive in school, he is being given special *assistance*. Normal disciplinary measures and procedures apply with children on these programmes, as with any children (correction, consequences, time-out or suspension).

> ***Behaviour recovery approaches?***
> *It's very time-consuming, especially in the initial stages, but the question we had to ask as a staff was, 'What's going to be the most advantageous … in the long run'. Yes, it is time-consuming but we had to consider how best we could use our time with stretched resources. How could we balance the teachers' needs (and support) with the rights of the other students, as well as the student with behaviour disorder.*
>
> *Jim: school principal*

Professional development

Many of the skills used by teachers in behaviour recovery are 'simply' effective teaching and management skills. The fine-tuning of such skills, including running classroom meetings, positive discipline practices, use of encouragement, even modelling and rehearsal, need to be part of a school's ongoing professional development. (Skills such as behaviour mirroring can be judiciously used, even in an after-class chat with students about behaviour! (Rogers 1998))

Teachers need the opportunity to talk about discipline concerns, to feel that it's professionally appropriate to share the angst that goes with managing challenging students and to have genuine opportunities and appropriate forums for problem-solving and planning workable support options, discipline practice (particularly consequences) and time-out programmes where necessary.

Conclusion

Essentially, behaviour recovery is a structured process within which students with behaviour needs can learn behaviours that will enable them to be more successful in behaviour and learning outcomes in school. It also aims, concurrently, to enhance positive self-esteem and the acceptance of personal responsibility. It is hoped, too, that these students will gain a more positive peer acceptance through modifying their behaviour.

Some children respond very quickly to behaviour recovery approaches, others will take a lot longer. If the support (or at least the understanding) of parents can be enlisted — even better. Schooling is a partnership between school and home, and parents need to take some responsibility for their children's behaviour at school.

For it to work behaviour recovery requires significant whole-school support and understanding. Students spend a third of their day at school, most of it with the class teacher as caregiver. In fact, for some students with emotional behaviour disorders the school and their teacher may well provide a significant, secure and sane place in their lives. At the end of the day it is the quality of this teacher–student relationship that will effect any change in disturbing and disordered behaviour. It is the quality of human interaction that will enable the programme to have any effect.

These students impose considerable strain on the limited resources of a school; there is no question that an increase in integration aides (or teachers) could be usefully allied to behaviour recovery training in schools.

There are few off-site units that primary age children can be enrolled for specialist support programmes and, in these days of integration into the mainstream (as the philosophic norm), schools are expected to take on almost every student. The fact is, anyway, that the number of such students exceeds the availability of off-site units, except in extreme cases.

Balancing the learning, welfare and behavioural concerns of *all* students at school is not easy, but programmes like behaviour recovery can assist by enabling these children to believe they can take positive control of their school experience.

Appendix: Photocopiable Masters

Introduction

The supplementary material is designed to be utilised within a whole-school approach to behaviour management for students with EBD. It is designed to be used in conjunction with the text, *Behaviour Recovery*, by providing teachers with a set of photocopy masters (PM) which focus on the more common behaviours of students with EBD. These PMs are a key focus in the teaching of positive social behaviours and can be used directly (photocopied) or with minor modifications to enhance the school's management goals for students with EBD.

Any intervention and support programme for such students is best developed using a team approach in order to facilitate analysis of the problem behaviours and the provision of ongoing moral and structural support and evaluation. This colleague support is essential; teachers should not be left merely to manage such students on their own.

The fundamental goals of all behaviour management are no different for children with EBD. The goals are:

- ownership of behaviour
- respecting of mutual rights
- building confidence in personal locus of control.

The student is given the same consistent treatment with regard to rules, rights, responsibilities and consequences as any other student, but often needs one-to-one assistance outside the classroom to enhance the behavioural goals outlined above.

Behaviour Recovery within a whole-school approach to behaviour management

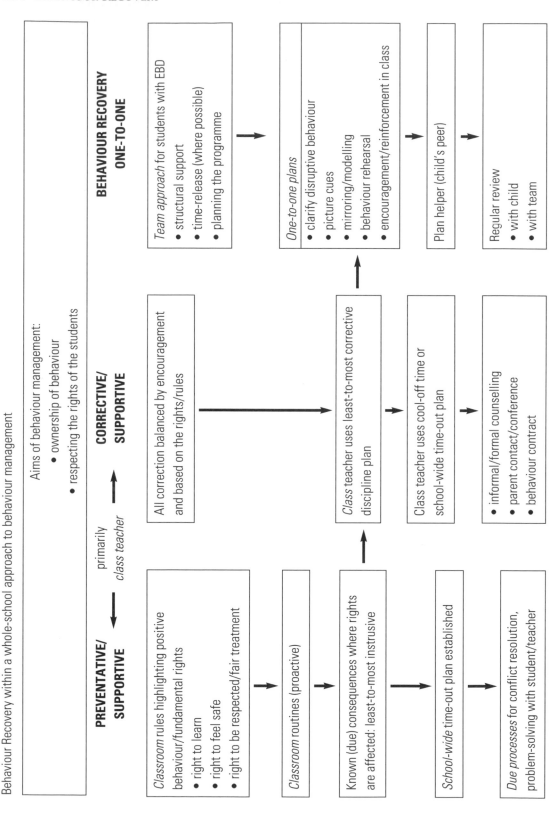

A whole-school approach

A framework for behaviour recovery within a whole-school approach is set out on page 154.

For behaviour recovery approaches to operate with any success it is important that each class teacher (and specialist teacher) has a common framework for classroom rights, responsibilities, rules and consequences. This provides consistency and a measure of reasonable certainty about how behaviour will be addressed. Rules are seen to be more effective when they are expressed simply and, as positively as possible, are few in number, clear and positive in expression, discussed with the students during the establishment phase of the year, and are then published (with cartoons or photos at lower/middle primary level). See Chapter 5.

Routines

It is also crucial to introduce clear, simple classroom routines for *all* students. Good routines provide positive preventative management and are best explained, discussed, taught, practised (where necessary) and enforced in the establishment phase of the year. Teach the routines for:

- line-up; entry/departure from classroom; mat-time; or settling to desks/tables; signals/cues for teacher attention and assistance, distribution and retrieval of materials; toilet/drink breaks, appropriate 'noise levels' (inside/partner voices) and so on (pp. 16 and 162).
- rotation of monitors
- procedures for quiet reading time
- pack-up, minimising clutter, maximising space
- access to cupboards, work stations resource areas and learning centres.

Consider the seating plan carefully. It can be helpful to place students with EBD closer to the front of the teaching location and near (or with) the more responsible and naturally co-operative students to minimise distraction. Plan a withdrawal area where students can be relocated if necessary and an in-class time-out area (see Chapter 6).

Discuss classroom routines, within a whole-school approach, as part of the school's preventative management plan. It may be helpful to utilise a common checklist for routines developed prior to the beginning of each year/term for each grade/subject team.

Consequences

All students need to know the consequences of rule-breaking. More importantly they need to know that when rules are broken the rights of others are affected. These consequences, like the rules, should be discussed, in the beginning of each new class and followed on after positive correction (see Chapter 6). In-class consequences (applied by class/specialist teacher) can include alternative tasks, relocation, cool-off time or staying back to help. In-class consequences should precede the use of time-out. Out-of-class consequences will range from detention to withdrawal of privileges through to suspension.

Once a classroom (as a social group) is established the class teacher can consolidate a number of activities to enhance group belonging: self-esteem activities; co-operative learning approaches; classroom meetings for problem-solving and general discussion (see Chapter 5); special class treats and free-time activities.

Thoughtful preventative measures and planned, positive corrective measures will go a long way to enhancing positive and responsible behaviour in most students. Some students, will need the special teaching that recovery-type approaches provide. The earlier such programmes are introduced to the student the more effective they will be.

Using the teaching cards (photocopy masters)

The supplementary material provides a number of pictorial *teaching cards* to help teachers plan the recovery sessions with their students. These cover the most commonly displayed distracting and disruptive behaviours; they are set out with the attendant on-task behaviours. These can be adapted to suit particular students by changing hair styles and clothing, adding freckles and asking the student to colour in the clothing.

Alternatively, teachers can draw up their own teaching cards (behaviour plans), or have a colleague draw them up prior to each rehearsal session. The class teacher could also enlist the drawing skills of an older student, or even the student himself.

Picture cues are a very important feature of the Behaviour Recovery programme. They provide:

- a concrete vehicle for teacher–student communication and a focus for the discussion of the student's behaviour
- an anchor for the child's understanding of off- and on-task behaviour

- a record of aspects of behaviour we wish to focus on (The tick-boxes at the bottom of the card allow a simple feedback mechanism that can back up teacher descriptive feedback.)
- a 'portable reminder' for the child to refer to during the day.

When using the card to begin a process of recovery be sure to:

- ask the child who he thinks the person in the picture is (The one out of his seat, or rolling on the mat, or calling out or ...)
- ask what he is doing
- ask him to focus on the faces (of the teacher and students) in the background: 'What can you tell me about them? What do you think they feel? What do you think they are thinking? Why?'

Clarify the social disapproval of his peers in the picture (the disruptive behaviour) because he is doing 'x', 'y' or 'z'. Do this with the following:

- 'What should you be doing?'
- 'Let's have a look at the next picture.'
- 'What are *you* doing in this picture?'
- 'What can you tell me about what the other students are thinking ... feeling ... why?'

This discussion clarifies the 'shape' of the current disruptive behaviour, the effect on others, and the desirability (as well as the hopeful prospect) of changing that behaviour. Remember to keep the tone positive, expectant and move on to the benefit of the plan as a way of gaining social approval and doing the right thing; observing the 'fair rule'. Utilising '*our*' fair rules as a focus further enhances the social aspect of positive behaviour. It can be helpful to have a copy of the relevant classroom rule to assist in the primary discussion of off-task and on-task behaviour.

The picture card is the child's reminder (see photocopy masters):

- ask him where he would like to keep his copy: in his desk, on the teacher's desk or in his locker
- keep a copy of the card yourself (he may lose it) and be sure to record on your copy whatever you mark on his. All support colleagues should also have a copy
- review it, at least initially, at the end of each timetable slot (The tick-boxes can be used to record the times when you noticed he remembered, and followed, his plan.)

The teacher(s) can also use the plan card as a reminder, or prompt, when the student 'forgets' his plan. As a management tool it can be referred to quickly without having a long discussion, yet again, about calling out, seat-wandering and so on. Show him the card (your copy) and use the short reminder, direction, or question and feedback (see Chapter 6).

Remember

- In the initial phase of the recovery programme the card(s) can display both off-task and on-task behaviour. The off-task behaviour can have a stop line through it to highlight 'Stop doing this'. This can be replaced with a teaching card illustrating the positive behaviour alone.
- Keep a copy for yourself, for specialist teachers, and senior staff (or team leader). Each card is a descriptive assessment, as well as a reminder for the child.
- The teaching card can be reduced to a portable student-sized card. Keep it in a transparent plastic envelope (or laminate it) and decide, with the student, where his copy will be located. **Note:** it is important that the student's copy of their plan is small enough not to be visually obtrusive to others (postcard sized).
- Evaluate the student's progress, with the card, daily.
- Teachers don't have to have a reward schedule built in (see tick-boxes at the bottom of each teaching card); the key feature of 'recovery' time is the teacher's one-to-one engagement in an out of class, and her regular descriptive feedback (p. 72).

PM1   The disruptive-behaviour profile

This profile can be taken over a seven-day cycle, initially, to assess the key factors of *frequency* and *intensity*, regarding the disruptive behaviours. There will often be a number of distracting and disruptive behaviours that can be isolated; it can be helpful to start with the most commonly disturbing in terms of frequency and intensity.

Keep a note (during class time) of the number of times the student, for instance, calls out, seat wanders, is inappropriately loud and rocks in his chair. It is important that these disruptive behaviours are specifically noted (in the left-hand column).

Frequency can be noted with ticks (the number of times he is disruptive), but it's naturally cumbersome carrying a form around all the time. Most teachers keep a small notebook and transfer the frequency count to the profile form at the end of the class session.

Intensity is difficult to measure. It is noted on the profile as a scale, 1–5, in order to measure how that behaviour affects you (as class teacher) and the other students. Of course, intensity can be affected by a teacher's bad-day syndrome too!

The initial profiling is used to enable the class teacher and the collegial team to identify the nature and extent of the problem behaviours. It can also be used, judiciously, with supportive parents to help clarify what is happening in class and what issues the recovery programme will attempt to address.

The profile addresses the disruptive behaviour in relation to time of day: before and after morning play (BMP/AMP) and after lunch and after afternoon recess (AL/AAR). If a pattern clearly emerges teachers can note what precedes that time of day (when *frequency* and *intensity* are noted as being more marked) and to see — further — if any changes to routine, teaching and learning, seating, or even links with home can be made. It is also helpful to note frequency and intensity during the two key phases of each class session, particularly the up-front time (UFT) when many attention-seekers monopolise the relative quiet attention expected of students as they focus on the teacher, the teaching, the task, or the demonstration.

PM 2   Blank card

This card has been prepared to simply allow a teacher to draw up a behaviour plan to suit a specific teaching situation.

The plan can be drawn up by any teacher, prior to the one-to-one sessions, as long as the visual representation is clear to the child. It could even be drawn up by the child himself — with teacher guidance — as part of the child's awareness raising.

The card is divided into two parts, allowing illustration space for both off-task and on-task behaviours. The small squares at the bottom of the page can be used as a tick and check record of on-task approximations.

PM 3   The programme outline

The flow chart has been duplicated from the text outlining the key phases and elements of the recovery programme. It can be used when preparing staff workshops and briefings, and as a focus/reminder for teachers involved in the programme.

The left side of the chart shows the basic phases of the programme in order of application. The chart highlights the key focus of these phases for each one-to-one recovery session. The last phase occurs, naturally, in the classroom (or wider school) setting; namely, the encouragement and feedback that occurs in the natural setting where the child has to behave considerately with his peers. The key phases are outlined in Chapter 3. The enlisting of a peer helper (a 'plan helper') is outlined in Chapter 4.

The right side of the chart shows the supportive elements of the programme:

- a behaviour profile, which is used to assist in diagnosis and ongoing evaluation (see Chapter 2, pp. 21–2, and PM 1)
- the team-support process, which is essential (see chapters 1, 6 and 8)
- the possible use of classroom meetings as a way of utilising the understanding and support of the student's peers (see Chapter 5)
- running records and evaluation, which are essential in any recovery programme. All teachers having duty-of-care (for example, specialist teachers) need to support the class teacher regarding feedback for running records. This can be achieved by using the behaviour profiles on a weekly basis (see PM 1).

The ongoing evaluation should be assessed on a team basis to determine whether or not the programme is effecting any behaviour change.

During on-task time (OTT) the class group is normally more focused on the learning requirement/task. Hence, with more working noise, acceptable movement, allocated attention to task, the student engaged in attention patterns of behaviour may well change the frequency and mode of his behaviour because the audience is more 'diffuse'.

It will be important to establish a daily profile, at least initially, to note whether the frequency and intensity of disruptive behaviour is changing with the introduction of the programme. Over a six- to eight-week period it is expected that there will be a reduction (sometimes a significant reduction) in the key factors of frequency and intensity. It is also important that support and specialist teachers profile each session they have with students on behaviour recovery programmes and feed this back to the class teacher. All profiling takes time, initially, but as part of an evaluative and support process it gives insight and shape to diagnosis, and monitoring and aids programme planning.

As noted in the text (see Chapters 2 and 8) any success as a result of the programme is seen in how the child approximates his behaviour to the plan: a drop in frequency and intensity of one kind of behaviour and an increase in another. Teachers (or parents) who expect an overnight change in disruptive and disordered behaviour 'expect' in vain. It is also impractical to assume there will be no further occurrence of calling out, butting in, seat-wandering or time off-task. It is the change in frequency and intensity of the 'old' patterns of behaviour that is the test of whether the one-to-one teaching of positive behaviour is having an effect. The major goal of this programme is the student's reasonably stable approximation to 'the norm' of behaviour expected within the child's age and development. And, most of all, an understanding (and hopefully belief) that he has a locus of control regarding his behaviour.

PM 4a 4b, 4c   Behaviours related to mat-time or together time

This behaviour is quite common with four- to seven-year-olds. Children can either be motorically restless, roll around (and make noises) or sit away from the group.

When utilising teaching plans for such students it is important to emphasise the social approval/disapproval in the picture cue. Teach the child to sit near you — as teacher — (even indicate a place) and rehearse this. Point out that you want him to sit near you because you can see him better and he can help you (by holding a book, a felt-tip pen and helping with materials), not because he is naughty. By having him sit at the front (quietly, without pushing in) he is less likely to be distracted.

PM 5   Seat-leaning at table/desk or frequent turning around

This behaviour can be common at any age level, especially with children who are easily distracted.

When utilising the teaching plan be sure the child knows what you mean by 'four-on-the-floor' and why it is important. Modelling is very effective here. Show him a privately understood signal (four fingers extended downwards as if four chair legs on the floor). Let him know this is a 'private' reminder to him if he forgets his plan.

For those students who turn around frequently, cue (privately understood signal) with finger to the eyes and then point ahead as if back to the work at hand. These signals can be given from a distance with a wink or smile. They are obviously best given with positive body language. They are brief, non-intrusive reminders, but they need to be taught during rehearsal time.

PM 6   Calling out, talking out of turn, inappropriate loudness in communication

This is probably the most common disruptive behaviour and one amenable to behaviour recovery. Students enjoy teachers noting (and noticing) the times when they have 'caught' the student observing the fair rule and behaving in a positive way. You can use the card to note both the talking out of turn and the inappropriate loudness. Remind the student that if he forgets his plan you will cue him in order to remind him. You can:

- put up your hand to remind of the hands-up rule or put your hand up and then four fingers to your mouth as if to say 'Hands-up without calling out' (at infant or lower primary)
- bring the forefinger and thumb together in a closing motion and then four fingers to the mouth to indicate 'Quieter voice, thanks' or 'partner-voice of table groups' (p. 16)
- turn down the imaginary volume control with thumb and forefinger.

Teach these signals in rehearsal time (pp. 48–9).

PM 7   Annoying, interfering with, distracting and/or hurting others

This is a common way of gaining attention from both peers and the teacher. It is important to relate this behaviour back to the class rule about feeling/being safe at school and the right of everyone to have the chance to learn without interruption.

All class members should know that it is OK to say, 'Stop it. I don't like it when …,' when other students interfere with their learning time.

While minor hassling can be *tactically* ignored, any significant infringement of safety and learning rights needs swift, brief reminders of the rule, relocation in the classroom or, with hostile and aggressive behaviours, immediate time-out (see Chapter 6).

During teaching/rehearsal sessions emphasise to the child that he cannot do these things (be specific with focused or general mirroring) because people do not feel safe and cannot learn. Emphasise the social disapproval aspect of such behaviour and re-focus on the positive benefits of time on-task, moving through the room without annoying others and using positive language. The plan can be termed 'Being kind to others', or

'My behaviour helps others'. Students are taught several specific ways to help others:

- walk from A to B without touching or hassling others or their work
- speak kindly
- remember 'Please'; 'Ta'; 'Thanks'; 'Can I borrow?'; 'Excuse me' when moving past someone's personal space; wait your turn; return things you've borrowed ...

Rehearse these behaviours and be ready to encourage the child when he demonstrates them in class.

PM 8   Seat-wandering, motoric restlessness (leaving seat without good reason)

This can be similar to the behaviour discussed in PM 7, depending on how intrusive the behaviour is. Some students wander due to habit, some because they are bored, some because they simply can't do the set work, for some it is a feature of ADD behaviour and a few because they are 'away with the fairies' as it were!

Emphasise to the child that this plan will help them get his work done in class. If a 'reward schedule' is used for this kind of plan it can be enhanced by a task/goal card on the child's desk to focus on set work times; it is a visual reminder (see PM 17c).

PM 9   Time on-task

This teaching plan is similar to PM 8 and may need to be taught in conjunction with it. There are several reasons why the student might be task-avoiding or task-refusing:

- inability or difficulty with the work; lack of understanding
- the tasks are often long or without enough structure
- no clear routine for starting the work (see pp. 74–6)
- short concentration span (a range of symptomatic ADD behaviours).

All these possibilities should be explored before considering a behaviour recovery plan.

Make sure the student knows what materials he will need at the table or desk. A small task card can be made up showing the materials required. If a particular work layout is required, be sure to have a sample he can refer to as well as a standard sample on a wall poster. It saves on the overuse of reminders.

It can be helpful with a younger student to use an egg-timer on his desk as a special reminder of time on-task (if he is willing). Let him know he needs to do his work while the sand is running down. When it stops he can put up his hand and you will come and check the work. If there is a plan helper he/she can fulfil that role. A three- to five-minute egg-timer is a useful start. Five minutes is quite a long time in relation to both time on-task and general motoric restlessness. Some of my colleagues use a three-minute egg-timer for a week, then switch to a five-minute egg-timer. There are also quiet, but audible, electronic timers. Such egg-timers are obviously used at infant age level with the child's permission.

PM 10   Gaining teacher attention inappropriately

These behaviours often result from low tolerance to frustration or attentional needs: 'Help me now!'

The student will often:

- call out or shout repeatedly
- butt in while you are helping another child
- pull at your clothes
- not wait in turn for marking.

The teaching card can focus directly on the rule for hands up and wait (or whatever the class rule is for getting teacher help in on-task learning time). Alternatively, if the teacher is happy with the student waiting near her (until she can give due attention) this, too, can become a 'target behaviour'.

You need to model how the student butts in, or pulls at your clothes (simulate this without touching the child simply by pulling at your own clothes or 'creating' an 'imaginary teacher'), then rehearse the student waiting near you until you say, 'Thanks for waiting'. Alternatively, rehearse hands up and waiting or whatever the appropriate teacher-attention procedure is. You can use privately understood signals to communicate target behaviours to the students (see Chapter 3). It is most important that you reinforce the on-task behaviour of the student and note it in class time and feedback time.

PM 11a   **Verbal aggression, physical destructiveness**
11b

It is important to distinguish between swearing directed at frustration and swearing as abuse (to either students or the teacher).

Frustration-engendered swearing needs a brief tuning in about how the student might be feeling and about good, positive or appropriate language in class. It doesn't need a lecture on morality. Teach him other words to use when angry (see Chapter 7). Swearing at a teacher can be in passing (sotto voce) or face-to-face; there is a difference. Both need recovery teaching time. Emphasise alternative words or actions.

Discuss with colleagues about exit/removal from class (for time-out) for verbal abuse, verbal threats of aggression, yelling or mouthing obscenities (see Chapter 6). Physical aggression should be met with immediate time-out; calmly and firmly. Behaviour plans for verbal or physical aggression need to focus on:

- distinguishing between legitimate feelings and unacceptable *behaviour*
- the safety/treatment rule
- how to manage anger (see Chapter 7)
- alternative words to use
- practising the anger management plan.

If you notice an increase of frustration in the child during class time, you can call him over and quietly remind him of the plan and/or of the consequences.

PM 12   **Anger management plan**

An anger management plan should be simple, using two or three steps learned in recovery time (see Chapter 7). The recovery teaching card provides a space for you to note down some key words or phrases for the student to remember his plan.

- 'I *feel* angry — remember the plan.'
- '*Relax*, breathe slowly' — relax muscles in the face, shoulders and hands …
- *Count* to ten (backwards from ten for older children: it's more cognitively demanding).

Recognise 'it' is coming, close the eyes, hands in the lap (or head in cradled arms), count to ten, breathe in/out slowly three times, relax the eye-brows, relax the 'screwed up' face, relax the hands and fingers, and shoulders. Say, 'I am slowing down my angry feelings'.

Some teachers teach the whole class basic stress-reducing exercises (this is good for the teacher as well!).

PM 13   Angry thoughts/angry behaviour

This card can be used in rehearsal time to teach the student about thinking and behaviour.

The card symbolises two kinds of thinking: both affect behaviour. Use discursive questions to teach the connection between different kinds of thinking and behaviour. Use the self-talk (think aloud, think quiet) ideas in Chapters 3 and 7 to show how helpful thoughts help behaviour to be more positive.

The 'CD' ideas are very useful, here, for older children (pp. 69 and 126).

PM 14   Helpful thoughts, helpful behaviour

This card can be used in rehearsal time and can also be used during a quiet spot in class time as a daily reminder in conjunction with the 'I can' reminder card (see PM 15).

PM 15a 15b   The 'I can' teaching card

These cards can be used on the child's table, in conjunction with rehearsal time, to remind them of the 'I can' messages relative to their behaviour plan. These cards are best introduced when there has been significant take-up of the on-task behaviour(s) that are part of the teaching plan. The card can symbolise a simple 'I can' message. The child can be encouraged to write his own 'I can' message in the think bubble. Examples include:

- I can put my hand up without calling out.
- I can move through the room without disturbing (or annoying) others.
- I can stay in my seat.
- I can speak in a quiet voice.

The 'think bubble' can also *pictorially* represent the 'I can' behaviour. The teacher reduces the positive on-task behaviour picture and locates it in the think bubble. If the child has difficulty reading an 'I can' or 'When/then' message a *picture* in the think bubble is a very positive, visual reminder.

PM 16a 16b   Take charge plan

The take-charge teaching cards are designed for non-assertive and overly assertive or bullying students at middle primary to middle school years.

The cards pictorially represent the difference between non-assertion, assertion and 'aggro' (aggro is a familiar term to children as an abbreviation for aggression; both words can be used).

The emphasis of the teaching cards is the difference between off-task (non-assertive) and on-task (assertive) behaviours. The on-task behaviours need to be taught as a 'need to take charge of my behaviour' plan. Emphasise to the student that only one person can really make him behave well, fairly, helpfully or (for non-assertive students) strongly — HIMSELF (see Chapter 7). The think bubbles for children who have been victims of bullying can include 'think strong', 'say strong' or 'look strong', with key phrases and body-language to practise. It goes without saying that the student needs to be willing to take on such recovery teaching.

PM 17a 17b, 17c   Contract cards

These simple contracts can be adapted to time on-task activities. The balls represent an aspect of the work completed relative to a set goal. This goal can be a set piece of work, a worksheet, a particular skill, even a *period of time* over which a skill or activity is pursued. The student can colour in each 'phrase' (the ball) towards the desired goal.

These cards are best utilised with task sheets (p. 74). A task sheet outlines the task for a particular literacy or numeracy activity. This is noted on a small folded card with twenty boxes; each box is shaded in (or ticked after a three- to five-minute time increment). Five- to six-year-olds can have an egg-timer placed on their table to guide them. If a plan helper is assisting the child (see Chapter 4) he/she can check the time on-task recording. When each task sheet is completed, a ball is coloured in on the main contract card. When all the 'balls' have reached their goal the student can receive a certificate, a 'free-time' activity or some pre-agreed celebration (rather than a *reward* as such) (see also PM 9).

**PM 18a
18b, 18c**

Anger diary/feeling thermometer

These cards provide a checklist/feedback mechanism between the teacher and the student. You will both have a copy of the plan and compare it with the student on a daily basis, or twice daily at infants. The checklist can be used as a diagnostic tool, as well as a recording device. In rehearsal time talk about anger, angry feelings and what can be done to control anger (see Chapter 7). Point out that it's not bad to get angry, but some people do silly, unhelpful, even bad things when they get angry; things that annoy others, make it difficult to learn or, even, hurt others.

Encourage the child to make a note in his anger diary whenever he feels himself getting angry. Describe the difference between being a little upset or annoyed and very angry. Use your hands to show him the 'size' of the feeling. The diary is to help him recognise and know his angry feelings, and to use this knowledge within his anger management plan (see PM 12).

The student can bring his anger diary/feeling thermometer to daily check-ups and rehearsal sessions to discuss how he is going. The diary is better suited to lower primary age children; the feeling thermometer for upper primary age children and the middle years.

PM 1

Behaviour Recovery
© Bill Rogers 2004

PROFILE: DISRUPTIVE BEHAVIOUR									
Name of Child:					**Date:**				
		AM				PM			
Off/On-task		BMP		AMP		AL		AAR	
behaviour	F/I	F	I	F	I	F	I	F	I
1 For example, calling out	UFT								
	OTT								
2 For example, inappropriate loudness in class	UFT								
	OTT								
3 For example, seat-wandering	UFT								
	OTT								

CODE

F	= Frequency of distruptions	AL	= After lunch
I	= Intensity (on a scale of 1–5)	AAR	= After-afternoon recess
BMP	= Before-morning play	UFT	= Upfront time
AMP	= After-morning play	OTT	= On-task time

PM 2

PM 3   Behaviour Recovery
© Bill Rogers 2004

Key phases and elements of the recovery programme

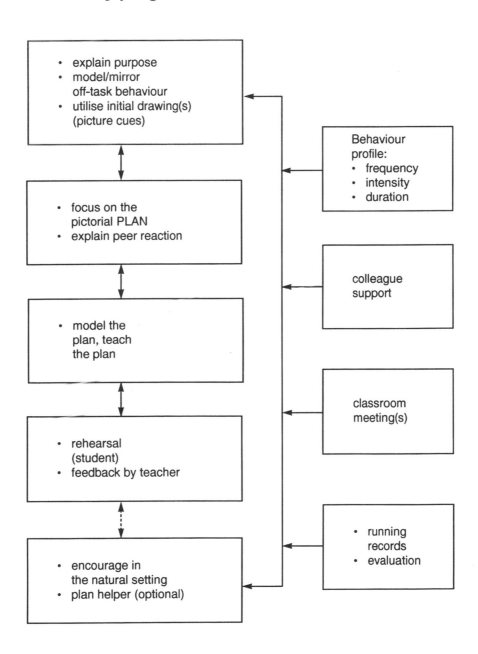

PM 4a

PM 4b Behaviour Recovery
© Bill Rogers 2004

PM 4c

PM 5 **Behaviour Recovery**
© Bill Rogers 2004

PM 6

PM 7 Behaviour Recovery
© Bill Rogers 2004

PM 8   Behaviour Recovery
© Bill Rogers 2004

PM 9 **Behaviour Recovery**
© Bill Rogers 2004

PM 10

Behaviour Recovery
© Bill Rogers 2004

PM 11a   **Behaviour Recovery**
© Bill Rogers 2004

PM 11b

Behaviour Recovery
© Bill Rogers 2004

PM 12　　　**Behaviour Recovery**
　　　　　　　© **Bill Rogers 2004**

PM 13　　　**Behaviour Recovery**
© Bill Rogers 2004

PM 15a   **Behaviour Recovery**
© **Bill Rogers 2004**

PM 16a   Behaviour Recovery
© Bill Rogers 2004

PM 17a **Behaviour Recovery**
© **Bill Rogers 2004**

PM 17b   **Behaviour Recovery**
© **Bill Rogers 2004**

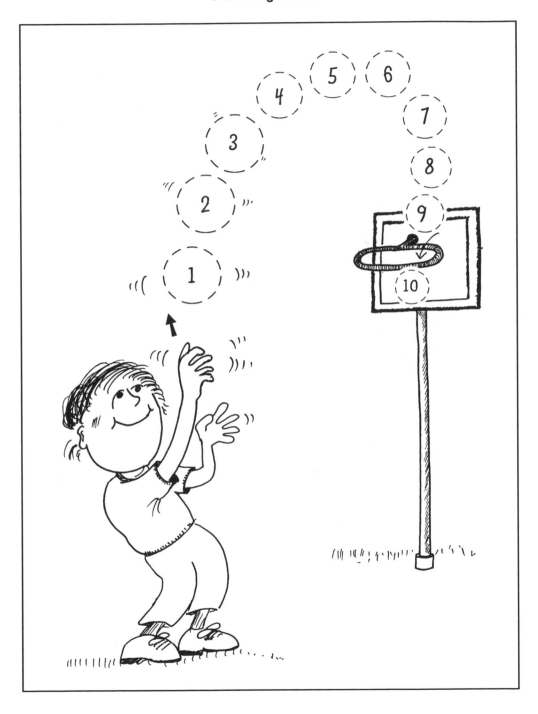

PM 17c   **Behaviour Recovery**
© Bill Rogers 2004

PM 18a   **Behaviour Recovery**
© **Bill Rogers 2004**

How I'm feeling . . .	M	T	W	Th	F

PM 18b   **Behaviour Recovery**
© **Bill Rogers 2004**

How I'm feeling...	M	T	W	Th	F

PM 18c   **Behaviour Recovery**
© Bill Rogers 2004

- When do I get angry?
- What do I get angry about?
- How angry am I?
- What can I do next time?

Bibliography

Acaster, D. 2000. *Strategies For Developing Empathy in Children: A Teacher–Parent Guide to Enhance Positive (and Reduce) Negative Behaviours*. Blackburn, Melbourne: Empathy Play.

Anderson, L.S. 1989. 'The aggressive child', *The Best of Set: Discipline*. Hawthorn, Victoria: ACER.

Bernard, M. & Joyce, M. 1984. *Rational Emotive Therapy with Children and Adolescents*. New York: J. Wiley & Sons.

Besag, V. 1989. *Bullies and Victims in Schools*. Milton Keynes, United Kingdom: Open University Press.

Boer, B. & Gleeson, V. 1982. *The Law of Education*. Sydney: Butterworth Press.

Borba, M. & Borba, C. 1982. *Self-esteem: A Classroom Affair*, vols 1 & 2, Melbourne: Dove Communications.

Braiker, H.B. 1989. The power of self-talk. *Psychology Today*, December, pp. 23–7.

Breheney, C., Mackrill, V. & Grady, N. 1996. *Making Peace at Mayfield: A Whole School Approach to Behaviour Management*, South Yarra, Victoria: Eleanor Curtain.

Cranfield, J. & Wells, H.C. 1976. *100 Ways to Enhance Self-concept in the Classroom*. New Jersey: Prentice-Hall.

Dempster, M. & Raff, D. 1992. *Class Discussions: A Powerful Classroom Strategy*. Cheltenham, Victoria: Hawker Brownlow Educational.

Dodge K.A. 1981. Social competence and aggressive behaviour in children. Paper presented to the Mid-western Psychological Association, Detroit, May.

Dodge, K.A. & Frame, C.L. 1982. Social cognitive biases and deficit in aggressive boys. *Child Development*, **53** p. 620–35.

Donaldson, M. 1978. *Children's Minds*. Glasgow: Fontana Collins.

Downing, C.J. 1986. Affirmations: steps to counter negative, self-fulfilling, prophesies. *Elementary and School Guidance and Counselling*, **20**, 175–9.

Dreikurs, R. 1968. *Psychology in the Classroom: A Manual for Teachers*, 2nd edn. New York: Harper & Row.

Dreikurs, R. 1985. *Happy Children: A Challenge to Parents*. Glasgow: Fontana.

Dreikurs, R., Grunwald, B. & Pepper, F. 1982. *Maintaining Sanity in the Classroom*, 2nd edn. New York: Harper & Row.

Ellis, A. & Bernard, M.E. (eds) 1983. *Rational-Emotive Approaches to the Problems in Childhood*. New York: Plenum Press.

Erikson, M.T. 1998. *Behaviour Disorders of Children and Adolescents: Etiology and Intervention*. New Jersey: Prentice-Hall.

Eron, L.D. 1987. The development of aggressive behaviour from the perspective of a developing behaviourism, *American Psychologist*, **5**: 435–42.

Faber, A. & Mazlish, E. 1980. *How to Talk So Kids Will Listen and Listen So Kids Will Talk*. New York: Avon Books.

Hall, J. 1993. *Confident Kids*. Melbourne: Lothian Books.

Harrison, J. 1991. *Understanding Children: Towards Positive Relationships*. Hawthorn, Victoria: ACER.

Howell, K. 1993. Eligibility and Need: Is There a Difference in Being Disturbed and Being Disturbing? In *Student Behaviour Problems: Positive Initiatives and New Frontiers*, ed. D. Evans, M. Myhill and J. Izard, Victoria: ACER.

Hutchins P. 1990. Biological perspectives on behaviour problems: an essential consideration for practical resolution. In *Practical Approaches to Resolving Behaviour Problems*, ed. S. Richardson & J. Izard Hawthorn, Victoria: ACER.

Hyndman, M. & Thorsborne, M. 1992. Bullying: a school focus. Paper presented to the Queensland Guidance and Counselling Association Conference, Queensland.

Kaplan, R.M., Konecini, V.J. & Novaco, R.W. 1984. *Aggression in Childhood and Youth*. The Hague: Nijhoff Publishing.

Knight, B.A. 1992. The roles of the student in mainstreaming. *Support for Learning*, **7** (4): 163–5.

Kyriacou, C. 1986. *Effective Teaching in Schools*: Oxford: Basil Blackwell, **7**: 55–60.

Kyriacou, C. 1991. *Essential Teaching Skills*. London: Basil Blackwell.

Macoby, E.E. & Jacklin, C.N. 1974. *The Psychology of Sex Differences*. California: Stanford University Press.

Macoby, E.E. & Jacklin, C.N. 1980. Sex differences in aggression: a rejoinder and reprise. *Child Development*, **51**: 964–80.

McGrath, H. & Francey, S. 1993. *Friendly Kids, Friendly Classrooms*. Melbourne: Longman Cheshire.

Meichenbaum, D. 1977. *Cognitive Behaviour Modification*. New York: Plenum Press.

Morgan, D.P. & Jenson, W.R. 1988. *Teaching Behaviourally Disordered Students: Preferred Practices*. Toronto: Merrill Pub. Co.

Nelson, J. 1981. *Positive Discipline*. New York: Ballantyne Books.

O'Brien, T. 1998. *Promoting Positive Behaviour*. London: David Fulton.

Olweus, D. 1978. *Aggression in the Schools: Bullies and Whipping Boys*. Washington DC: Hemisphere.

Pikas, A. 1991. A pure concept of mobbing given the best results for treatment. In *Practical Approaches to Bullying*, P.K. Smith & D. Thompson London: David Fulton.

Nabukoza, D. & Smith, P.K. 1992. Bullying in schools: mainstream and special needs. *Support for Learning*, 7(1): 3–7.

Poteet, J.A. 1973. *Behaviour Modification: A Practical Guide for Teachers*. London: University of London Press.

Rickard, J. 1994. *Relaxation for Children*. Melbourne: ACER Press.

Rigby, K. 1996. *Bullying in Schools and What to Do About It*. Melbourne: ACER Press.

Rigby, K. & Slee, R. 1993. *Bullying in Schools* (video recording and instruction manual). Hawthorn, Victoria: ACER.

Robertson, J. 1989. *Effective Classroom Control — Understanding Teacher–Pupil Relationships*, 2nd edn. London: Hodder & Stoughton.

Rogers, B. 1985. *Conflict Resolution Among Pre-Adolescents*. Unpublished Masters Thesis, The University of Melbourne.

Rogers, B. 1992. Early intervention programmemes for behaviourally disordered students in mainstream school. In *Student Behaviour Problems: Directions, Perspectives and Expectations*, ed. B. Willis & J. Izard, Hawthorn, Victoria: ACER.

Rogers, B. 1993. Taming bullies — a whole-school focus. *Classroom*, May, pp. 12–15.

Rogers, B. 1995. *Behaviour Management: A Whole-School Approach*. Sydney: Scholastic Press.

Rogers, B. 1997. *Cracking The Hard Class: Strategies for Managing the 'Harder than Average' Class*. Sydney: Scolastic Press.

Rogers, B. 1998. *You Know the Fair Rule*: Victoria: ACER.

Rogers, B. 2002. *I Get By With a Little Help, Colleague Suport in Schools*. Camberwell: ACER Press.

Rogers, B. (ed.) 2004. *How to Manage Children's Challenging Behaviour*. London: Paul Chapman Publishing.

Rosenthal, R. & Jacobsen, L.F. 1967. Teacher expectations for the disadvantaged. Readings from *Scientific American*, San Francisco: W.F. Freeman & Co.

Rubin, K. & Pepler, D. (eds) 1991. *The Development and Treatment of Childhood Aggression*. Hillsdale. New Jersey: Erlbaum.

Rutter, M., Maughan, B., Mortimore, P. & Ouston J. 1979. *Fifteen Thousand Hours*. London: Open Books.

Seligman, M. 1991. *Learned Optimism*. Sydney: Random House.

Serfontein, G. 1990. *The Hidden Handicap: How to Help Children who Suffer from Dyslexia, Hyperactivity and Learning Difficulties*. Sydney: Simon & Schuster.

Silberman, C.F. 1970. *Crisis in the Classroom*. New York: Random House.

Slee, P. 1992. Peer victimisation at school: you can run, but you can't hide. Paper presented to the Behaviour Problems Conference, ANU, Canberra.

Smith, P. K. & Thompson, D. (eds) 1991. *Practical Approaches to Bullying*. London: David Fulton.

Stones, R. 1991. *No More Bullying*. London: Dinosaur Press (Harper Collins).

Van Houten, R. 1980. *Learning through Feedback*. New York: Human Sciences Press.

Wheldhall, K. (ed.) 1991. *Discipline in Schools: Psychological Perspectives on the Elton Report*. London: Routledge.

Wolpe, J. & Lazarus, A. 1966. *Behaviour Therapy Techniques*. Oxford: Pergammon Press.

Wragg, J. 1989. *Talk Sense to Yourself: A Program for Children and Adolescents*. Hawthorn, Victoria: ACER.

Subject Index

Author Index